STAND UP for YOUR RIGHTS

Editors at first editorial meeting:
Jasper Bakyayita, Uganda
Vivek Guha, India
Christine Jasinski, Belgium
Alejandro Jiménez Cabal, Mexico
Bremley W. B. Lyngdoh, India
Daniel Juwel Ngungoh, Cameroon
Joseph Robert, France
Leah Thigpen, USA
Lissa Wheen, UK

Editors at second editorial meeting:
Toyin Ajasa-Oluwa, UK
Paul Atgwa, Kenya
Damien Boltauzer, Canada
Gözde Boğa, Turkey
Alberto Granada, Colombia
Sheku Syl Kamara, Sierra Leone
Sayed Mosediq, Afghanistan
Alexander Woollcombe, UK
Jeta Xharra, Kosovo

Design and illustration team:
Urjana Shrestha, Nepal
Sanid Zuko, Bosnia-Herzegovina
Jantien Roozenburg, The Netherlands
Arshak Sarkissian, Armenia
Riffat Lotia, Pakistan

We would like to thank the following for their generous support of this project:
The Ministry of Foreign Affairs of The Netherlands;
The MacArthur Foundation; The Samuel Rubin Foundation;
The Reuters Foundation; The Polden-Puckham Charitable Foundation;
The Body Shop Foundation; The Armenian General Benevolent Union;
The Positive Spirit Network

Thanks also to Amnesty International, Anti-Slavery International, Children of the Andes,
Gerison Lansdown, Margot Brown, Tina Jorgensen, Tom Jolly, Dan Jones, Rupert
Woollcombe, Eirwen Harbottle and Richard Wheen for their help and advice,
to the Bob Marley Foundation for allowing us to include the lyrics of the song
'Get Up, Stand Up' and IPM, as exclusive licensor of the King Estate,
for the Martin Luther King quote.

Peace Child International
Project co-ordinator: Rosey Simonds
Youth project co-ordinator: Esther Vivas Esteve
Designer: Julian Olivier
Editorial adviser: David Woollcombe

Two-Can Publishing
Editorial Director: Jane Wilsher
Art Director: Belinda Webster
Production Director: Lorraine Estelle
Editorial support: Lucy Arnold, Leila Peerun

First published in 1998 by Two-Can Publishing Ltd,
346 Old Street, London EC1V 9RB.

Copyright © Peace Child International 1998,
The White House, Buntingford, Herts SG9 9AH, UK
British Registered Charity No. 284731

Dewey Decimal Classification 323
Hardback ISBN 1-85434-631-8
Paperback ISBN 1-85434-573-7

A catalogue record for this book is available
from the British Library.

Printed in Spain by Graficas Reunidas

Photographic credits
p4 Supplied by the UN High Commission for Refugees; p14 Supplied by the UN;
p27 Both supplied by Anti-Slavery International; p31 Supplied by the South African High
Commission for Refugees; p34 Supplied by Amnesty International; p40 Photo by Visar
Krueziu; p48 Supplied by Amnesty International; p50 Supplied by Michael Aris;
p84 Photo of Kosovo demonstration by Visar Krueziu.
All other photographs were taken by the young contributors.

Front cover illustration: Jantien Roozenburg, 15, The Netherlands
Illustrations for Article headings: Urjana Shrestha, 18, Nepal
Map p6-7: Mel Pickering

Publisher's note

This book represents a year's work by the young members of the Peace Child International network. They gathered facts, interviews, opinions, stories, poems and photographs from young people all around the world. This material was then pulled together by a group of young editors to provide fresh perspectives and a commentary on the Declaration of Human Rights.

Each Article of the Declaration is summarized, but some Articles are dealt with in more detail than others. The editors ask questions about the issues and highlight aspects with original material from the young contributors, along with their own editorial comment. The book reflects their own ideas and opinions based on their personal experiences, but final decisions on what was included in the book were made by the publishers.

The writing is often intensely personal. However, this thought-provoking material makes an excellent starting point for discussions about human rights both in and out of the classroom. The final pages are filled with opportunities for action and contacts for organizations that are involved in trying to fight for a free and fair world. The reference section is useful for teachers, particularly pages 80–81.

The publishers made every effort to verify the facts, but not all information could be substantiated, especially that given in personal accounts. The views and opinions of the contributors are not necessarily those of the publishers, the United Nations or any other organization mentioned.

'Human Chain' by Srijana Shrestha, 15, Nepal

Contents

Foreword

by Mary Robinson, UN High Commissioner for Human Rights

The objective of all human-rights action is simply this: to ensure a life of dignity for each person on this earth. The question is how? What makes sense to people who live a comfortable, secure life may make no sense at all to those living on the margins of society. This is a problem I am aware of every day in my job. I find that two words help me a lot in dealing with this problem: 'respect' – really listening and hearing each side's point of view – and 'responsibility' – finding the balance between securing my own rights and learning to live by them responsibly so that someone else is not deprived of their rights.

Another word I use often is 'together'. I believe the old Native American saying: "The hurt of one is the hurt of all". A single abused child is a scar on the face of the global family. Our lives will not be completely dignified until we can all achieve a basic level of dignity.

This is a difficult task. Your generation faces the most daunting challenges as we move into the new millennium: trafficking in children, environmental destruction, civil wars, corruption, inequality, nuclear proliferation. I believe we can only tackle all of these if we build our society on a solid foundation of human rights. Our approach must be directed by the principles that you will read about in these pages – the principles of the Universal Declaration of Human Rights – which are as relevant today as when they were adopted 50 years ago.

Human-rights work never stops. Many laws and treaties have been passed, but they need to be implemented. We must always be vigilant. Fifty years ago, children did not talk much about human rights – in fact, most people did not talk about them in the way we do today. Now, thanks to the work done since then and to television and the Internet, we can know immediately when someone's rights are being abused, even if it is far away. Yet abuses continue, which is why this project is so important. You are starting now on the road to defend your rights and the rights of children like you around the world.

I congratulate the young authors of this book for their dedication in educating themselves about human rights. You will read a lot of depressing stories here, but you will also read of heroism. Yes, we have come a long way in the last 50 years – apartheid and colonialism have almost disappeared and more people are expressing themselves freely than at any other time in history. You should celebrate the achievements, while acknowledging how far we still have to go. You are taking the first step by picking up this book. Learning about human rights is essential, but you must remember the steps that follow: to live by a philosophy of human rights and to work to secure them for everyone.
Mary Robinson

A message **from the editors**

Hi friends

We're so happy that you are sitting down to read our book because we, the editors, have had such a good time editing and designing it. Usually books like this are written by so-called experts – but not this one. More than 8,000 young people from 45 countries helped to make it – from Korea to Costa Rica, and from South Africa to Finland. We hope it reflects the ideas and dreams of each and every one.

Then, in July 1998, we – the lucky ones chosen to be the final editors – arrived here at the White House in England to review all the material and to prepare the book for the printers. It was not always easy. Even within our own group, there were different opinions about what human rights are. This made the experience something extraordinary. By respecting our differences, we realized that we all agree on one thing – we all strongly believe that everyone should have equal human rights.

We should explain how this book came about, because it's not like a normal book. Back in 1993, several young people got together over lunch at a UN Human Rights Conference in Vienna. They thought what a good idea it would be for young people everywhere to write about human rights. So they sent thousands of workbooks to schools, young people and youth groups world-wide, asking them to send in poems, reports and pictures – all about human rights. In April 1998, eleven young editors from nine countries sorted out the material. They put together a first draft of the book, which was sent to all the contributors for their comments. It was also sent to a team of human-rights educators and experts for review and guidance.

Now that you know how this book was made, we hope you enjoy the result. Working on it has made us really positive about making our world a better place.

The editors

5

Thanks to **everybody**

We would like to say a big thank you to all the people who sent in material for this book. As you can see from this map, the contributors come from all over the planet. There were so many different stories, pictures and case studies that it was impossible to include them all. We tried our best to make sure that we included a wide variety of ideas from different parts of the world. We also used lots of the submitted material for research when we were writing up stories.

Listed below are the names of the groups that took part in 'Stand Up for Your Rights'. Without them none of this would have happened.

AFGHANISTAN
NATURE, Afghanistan

ALGERIA
Peace Child International – Algeria

ARGENTINA
Andrés López, Argentina
Asociación para el Progreso de la Educación,
    Argentina
Escuela No. 12 Cornelio Saavedra, Argentina
Escuela No. 23 Almafuerte, Argentina
Escuela No. 34 Dra. Carolina Tobar Garciá,
    Argentina
Escuela No. 37 Bernardino Rivadavia, Argentina
Escuela No. 66 SES Quincentenario de la
    Independencia Argentina, Argentina
Escuela San Patricio, Argentina
Misión Rescate-Argentina, Argentina
Pamela Castro, Argentina
Team Work, Argentina
Valeria Gilardone, Argentina
Instituto de Secundaria Saúl Taborda, Argentina

AUSTRALIA
Oz Child, Australia

BENIN
Mission Terre-Benin, Benin

BOSNIA-HERZEGOVINA
Saburina Primary School, Bosnia-Herzegovina
The First Bosniak High School, Bosnia-Herzegovina

BURKINA FASO
Association de Protection et de Sauvegarde de
    l'Enfance en Danger, Burkina Faso

CAMEROON
Rescue Mission-Cameroon, Cameroon
The Environmental Club, Cameroon

CANADA
Spruce Glen Public School, Canada
Whycocomagh Consolidated School, Canada

COMORES
Sitti Fatouma Ahmed, Comores

COSTA RICA
Casa Alianza-Regional Office, Costa Rica
Centro Educativo Campestre, Costa Rica

CYPRUS
CYN Magosa Sub-Group, Cyprus
CYN English School, Cyprus

CZECH REPUBLIC
The Slavonic High School, Czech Republic
UNESCO Club Olomouc, Czech Republic

DEMOCRATIC REPUBLIC OF THE CONGO
Collège AH 12 Septembre, Democratic Republic of
    the Congo

FINLAND
Ethics 5-6 Roihuvuori Primary School, Finland
Puolalanmäki Agenda 21 Group, Finland

FRANCE
CM2 Ronchece, France
Collège Blaise Pascal, France

GAMBIA
Baroteh Primary School, Gambia
Kotu Senior Secondary School, Gambia
Rescue Mission Sub-Group Advocating for Human
    Rights, Gambia

GEORGIA
School No.122, Georgia

GERMANY
UNESCO Projekt Schule, Germany

GHANA
Accra Academy, Ghana
Accra High School, Ghana
Deks Junior Secondary School, Ghana
Eco Club of the Earth, Ghana
Rescue Mission-Ghana, Ghana

INDIA
Bhima Sangha, India
Child Association to Renascence to Earth (CARE),
    India

Consortium of Indian Scientists for Sustainable
    Development, India
Free the Children-India, India
Maharaja Sawai Man Singh Vidyalaya, India
Mahila Akta Samiti & Srijan, India
The Concerned for Working Children, India

INDONESIA
KKSP Foundation, Indonesia

KENYA
Environmental Club, Kenya
Environmental Protection and Community
    Development, Kenya
KURM, Kenya
Wamba Secondary School, Kenya

LITHUANIA
Silainiai Secondary School, Lithuania

MACEDONIA
First Children's Embassy in the World, Macedonia

MEXICO
Misión Rescate-Mexico, Mexico

NEPAL
Kathmandu Group, Nepal
Peace Child Nepal, Nepal

THE NETHERLANDS
Gymnasium Haganum, The Netherlands

Elena Noguera i Pigem, Spain
Escola Joan Pelegrí, Spain

SRI LANKA
Interactive Media Group, Sri Lanka

SWEDEN
Bagarmossens Skola 3A, Sweden

SWITZERLAND
Collège du Léman, Switzerland
International School Geneva, Switzerland

TOGO
Club Ecolo-Pacifiste, Togo

TURKEY
Turkey Mission, Turkey
Turkish Club of Human Rights, Turkey

UGANDA
Children's Advocates, Uganda
Naddangira Mixed Child Rights Club, Uganda
Nsangi Primary School, Uganda
Rescue Mission-Uganda, Uganda
St. John Bosco Katende Primary School,
   Uganda
The African Network for Prevention and
   Protection Against Child Abuse and
   Neglect, Uganda

UK
Fallibroome High School, UK
Fulford Amnesty Group, UK
George Mitchell School, UK
King Manor School, UK
Mill Mead School, UK
Newminster Middle School, UK
Saint Mary's School, UK
Trinity Junior School, UK
Ward Freeman School, UK

USA
Beasley Academic Centre, USA
Decatur Classical School, USA
Evergreen Academy, USA
Garrett A. Morgan Elementary School, USA
Girls Inc. USA
Ira F. Aldridge Elementary School, USA
Kenwood High School, USA
Lane Technical High School, USA
Lenart School, USA
Maria Saucedo Scholastic Academy, USA
Nash School, USA
Newberry Academy, USA
Ray School, USA
Robert Heahs Elementary, USA
Vanderpoel School, USA

YUGOSLAVIA
Postpessimists, Yugoslavia
United Games, Yugoslavia

NIGERIA
Child Rights Club, Nigeria
Ebonite Foundation, Nigeria
Nigeria Society for the Improvement of Rural
   People, Nigeria
YIELD, Nigeria

PAKISTAN
ABSA (school for deaf), Pakistan
Al-Madrassa-tul-Saifiya-tul Burhania, Pakistan
Bay View High School, Pakistan
Beaconhouse Public School, Pakistan
C.A.S. School, Pakistan
City School, Pakistan
Foundation Public School, Pakistan
Habib Girls' School, Pakistan
Happy Home School, Pakistan
Human Rights Education Programme, Pakistan
Nasra Secondary School, Pakistan
Pakistan Environmental Lobbying Society,
   Pakistan
St. Joseph's Convent School, Pakistan

PALESTINE
Green Peace Association, Palestine

PERU
Asociación ECOBOY, Peru
Asociación Pukllasunchis, Peru
Centro de Investigación y Desarrollo de la
   Educación, Peru

Colegio Jose Antonio Encinas, Peru
Grupo SAYWITE, Peru
Lima Young Persons Agenda 21 (LYPA 21), Peru
L@s niñ@s y jovenes de San Francisco, Peru
Misión Rescate-Peru, Peru
Tierra Vida, Peru

PHILIPPINES
Badian National High School, Philippines
Children and Peace Philippines, Philippines
Samahan ng mga Anak ng Desaparecidos,
   Philippines

RUSSIA
Physico-Technical Lyceum #1, Russia

SENEGAL
Défense des Enfants International Section 1,
   Senegal
Ecole de Formation G. Legoff, Senegal

SOUTH AFRICA
Realitivity, South Africa
Rescue Mission Gimmies, South Africa

SOUTH KOREA
Sarangbang Group for Human Rights,
   South Korea

SPAIN
Collegi Sant Andreu, Spain
Defensa de Niños y Niñas Internacional, Spain

Get up, stand up... read on

Do you know what your rights are? Did you know that over 150 governments have made an agreement that everyone has the right to life, that you can't lock up people without a proper trial, that you are free to practise whatever religion you want and much more? In 1948, the governments of the world came together in Geneva and agreed to the 'Universal Declaration of Human Rights', the document that sets out the rights to which everyone is entitled.

This book celebrates the 50th birthday of the Universal Declaration of Human Rights. In its 30 Articles, the Declaration defines the meaning and value of life. It is not just for people living in far-away places, in war zones or under oppressive dictatorships: it is about us, about the way we live our lives! Many feel it is the most important document the United Nations has ever produced.

As we started to work on this book, we realized that the issue of human rights is complicated. All sorts of problems and questions arose. Firstly, a problem – many people think that human rights are a luxury of prosperous countries. Which is more important – that a country observes human-rights laws or that its people have jobs, homes and enough to eat? Some countries also feel that Non-Governmental Organizations (NGOs) and the UN act like a human-rights police force which is ignorant of the causes of problems and throws out traditions that have served for thousands of years.

Then there is the question of how human rights should be enforced. Recently, there was an agreement to set up an international criminal court to punish leaders of countries who abuse the human rights of their citizens. But in the past, the power of such courts has proved limited.

We decided that the most straightforward and effective way of thinking about and enforcing human rights is to believe in them and teach them, to live by them every day and to stand up for them if need be.

We soon began to wonder what to call this book. There were plenty of ideas, but in the end we went for Stand Up for Your Rights from the famous song 'Get Up, Stand Up' by Bob Marley. Here are just a few lines:

Picture by Jantien Roozenburg, 15, The Netherlands

*Most people think great God will come
from the sky,
Take away ev'rything, and make
evr'ybody feel high,
But if you know what life is worth,
You would look for yours on earth.
And now you see the light,
You stand up for your right, yah!*

*So you'd better get up, stand up,
Stand up for your right.
Get up, stand up,
Don't give up the fight.*

About this book

In this book we've divided the Declaration into two broad sections and explored each of its 30 Articles in turn. The Articles in Part One deal with legal and political issues, such as freedom and equality for all people. Part Two addresses more specific themes relating to the day-to-day quality of life of an individual. We've written out each Article in plain English at the top of the page. You can find the original wording at the back of the book, on pages 90–91, along with the Convention on the Rights of the Child on pages 92–93. This looks at human-rights issues that particularly concern children.

Wherever possible we have credited articles and illustrations to the individual contributor and given his or her age, but unfortunately we did not always have this information.

You will find several different types of writing on these pages.
The introduction for each Article is written in bold type.
Passages reported by us in the third person are in plain type.
" Other passages, written in italics and contained within quotation marks, are direct accounts in the first person. "
Fictional stories and poems are signalled by the use of italics without quotation marks.
You can look up difficult words in our jargon buster at the end of the book, on pages 94–95.

In many ways, we think the back of the book is just as important as the front. Here, you can find out about groups that have challenged abuses of human rights, and changed the world forever. You'll also find details of how to get involved. It's time to change our world and make it a much better place. It's up to us to make it happen – NOW!

Our dreams...

We allowed ourselves to dream of a world in the future where all human rights are observed. Each of our dreams was different but there were certain common themes. Dreams are essential if we want to build a better world. By dreaming, we work out what we really want. These dreams can become our ideal and change the way we lead our lives.

Martin Luther King, the famous American civil-rights campaigner, dreamed of a society where everyone was equal. He believed the only way to make this dream come true was through non-violent struggle. One of our editors based the poem below on his 'dream'. (To find out more about Martin Luther King, turn to page 30.)

I have a dream

I have a dream
to fight for the rights of the people
I have a dream
to make our environment clean and green
I have a dream
of good education for children
I have a dream
to fly free as a bird.

I have a dream
to make friends of every race
I have a dream
to get peace in the world
I have a dream
not to have war anywhere
I have a dream
to eliminate world poverty.

I have a dream
I have lots of dreams...
I want every dream to come true –
But how?
Let's march forward hand in hand
and shoulder to shoulder
To make everyone's dream
come true!!!

Urjana Shrestha, 18, Nepal

One day...

Youngsters will learn words they will not understand.
Children in India will ask: What is hunger?
Children from Alabama will ask: What is racial segregation?
Children from Hiroshima will ask: What is the atomic bomb?
Children at school will ask: What is war?
You will answer them. You will tell them:
Those words are not used any more.
Like stage coaches, galleys or slavery.
Words no longer meaningful.
That is why they have been removed from dictionaries.

Martin Luther King

Human rights have a long history, which is often dominated by the abuse of rights, rather than by observance. Turn to the next page and travel with us down the road that led to the Universal Declaration in 1948, then see what has happened since.

Illustration by Urjana Shrestha, 18, Nepal

The **highs** and **lows** of human rights

The Magna Carta, signed in Britain in 1215, was the first attempt by a people to limit the divine right of kings. In 1689, the Bill of Rights improved on it by allowing kings to rule only by the wish of the people.

From the time of Moses, around the 14th century BC, laws were written down to defend human rights through courts of law.

In 300 BC, in ancient Greece, Antigone stood up for her rights. She disobeyed King Creon to give her brother a decent burial.

In some cultures, religion provided an excuse for abuse of human rights: inquisitions, fatwahs, sati and the practice of human sacrifice justified official killings.

Colonial expansion: beginning in the 15th century, powerful European nations created empires in Africa, Asia, Latin America and Oceania, removing all the human rights of the people who lived there.

Slavery: the worst abuse of human rights was the purchase of people as slaves. From the 16th century, Africans were transported in appalling conditions to work in the Americas. Many died as a result.

End of empires: in the 19th century Simon Bolivar led South America to independence. Gandhi helped India to independence in 1947 and by the early 1960s, most of the rest of the world was decolonized.

1990: The release of Nelson Mandela marked the beginning of the end of apartheid and of human rights' abuse for millions of black people.

1948: the Universal Declaration of Human Rights was signed by the UN. It was drawn up by an international committee chaired by USA ex-First Lady, Eleanor Roosevelt.

Karl Marx hoped communism would give power and rights to the people. In practice it often gave power to dictators like Stalin, who ruled the USSR throughout the 1930s and 1940s.

Symbolic barrier to human rights in Eastern Europe, the Berlin Wall, fell in November 1989. The end of communism brought greater freedom, but also new problems, to millions.

Illustration by Michael Troukades, 17, Cyprus

▼ START HERE

Human rights are as old as human beings. Stone-age families had rights and responsibilities.

Kings and tribal chiefs achieved their authority by birth, wealth or physical strength. They used their power to usurp the natural rights of their people.

French Revolution: the greatest revolt against the divine right of kings came in 1793 when the people of France adopted their Declaration of the Rights of Man. They guillotined the King and members of the French aristocracy.

Two brave slaves rebelled on their way to the Americas on a ship called the Amistad. They freed themselves and the other slaves. In 1841, an American court decided that these slaves were people, not property.

American Revolution (1775–1783): North America broke free from British rule and declared independence!

UNIVERSAL EDUCATION

Universal education: 19th-century Europeans used child labourers until they saw the economic benefit of an educated work-force.

The American Civil War (1861–1865) was fought over the issue of slavery. It started a long battle to eliminate slavery from the western world.

WHITES ONLY

Rights of women: in the UK, women first won the right to vote in 1918, after a brutal struggle. One woman threw herself to her death under the King's horse at the Derby.

Apartheid and segregation: slavery was replaced by a new and insidious way of judging people by the colour of their skin. Apartheid divided South Africans into first- and second-class citizens between 1948 and 1991.

Eleanor Roosevelt and how the Universal Declaration was signed

Eleanor Roosevelt, widow of former USA president Franklin D. Roosevelt, was elected chair of the United Nations Commission that wrote the Universal Declaration. Paid the princely sum of $15 a day, plus a subway ticket, she and her colleagues tried to define what is really meant by 'human rights'. The fact they agreed at all, and at a speed amazing to modern diplomats, was largely due to the personality and negotiation skills of Mrs Roosevelt. She hoped the Declaration would be a 'Magna Carta of all men everywhere' – and note the word 'men'. In fact, the only change we recommend be made immediately to the Declaration is to replace all the male pronouns with 'he/she', 'him/her' and so on.

Then, as now, the great debate was about how far international concern for human rights should be able to influence governments around the world. The Declaration neatly side-steps this issue by stating simply and boldly what human rights are, and not saying how they should be enforced.

Eleanor Roosevelt reviews her 'Magna Carta of all men', New York, December 1948.

The Universal Declaration of Human Rights
Part One

Civil and political rights
The basic right to freedom and equality

We are all **free** and **equal**

ARTICLE 1 MADE SIMPLE

All human beings are born free and have equal rights.

Everyone has reason and a conscience and should therefore be friendly to one another.

For many, many years, people have often thought that they are much smarter, much brainier, more good-looking, more cultured, funnier and generally better than other people. Surely that's pure arrogance. The reality is that nobody is 'better' than anyone else, we are all equal. Each person, each country, each town, each people has things that make it special.

In the same way it's also wrong to think that you can own anyone. You can't because everyone is free.

You may be wondering how on earth you make people respect one another and each other's rights when so many wars are going on around the world. Well, for us the only answer is knowledge and education. If we learn about our rights and about other people and cultures, then we can live together in peace.

The key to knowing

You have need of a key to know.
Liberty of thought is the fundamental right
And education is the universal key
To unlock the knowledge and wisdom
That lies in our books and in our history.

Every child, every human being has
A right to that key, for we all have a right
To build our lives on the knowledge
Accumulated by those who lived before us.
Without that key, our world is dark and choiceless.

A free world is one where every child has the
Key to a school.

Alberto Granada, 17, Colombia

Picture by Cory Adams, USA

Don't discriminate

ARTICLE 2 MADE SIMPLE

Everyone, whatever their race, colour, nationality, sex, political or other beliefs, however much money or property they have, and no matter what the strength or the politics of their national government, is entitled to the same human rights.

Humans are very quick to discriminate against, or judge, anyone who seems different. Have you ever been discriminated against because of your sex or where you come from? And if you really think about it, you've probably made judgements about people based solely on their appearance!

Article 2 is about racism, nationality and gender, but it fails to mention discrimination against disabled people or gays and lesbians. We were sent so much information on this Article that it was hard to restrict ourselves to just six pages! We apologize to everyone whose contributions we had to leave out.

I never knew what racism was about until I left my country

" *When I travelled from Sierra Leone to London through Belgium, my passport was taken even though I had the necessary travel documents like everyone else. I was taken aside and interrogated while all the white people passed through easily. I was shocked and felt humiliated as a black man.*

This was the first in a series of racist encounters for me. I was staying with a family in Buntingford, a small town north of London. One evening I went for a walk around the town. After 45 minutes, a police van stopped alongside me and a policeman got out, saying, "We have had a call reporting that a strange person was moving around". His statement took me aback. Then I asked myself, "Is it because I am black?"

My third encounter was late one night in London when I needed a taxi cab to take me home. Ironically, none of the taxis I stopped would take me on board. As I stood there, with the money for the fare in my pocket, I watched the white people go off home while I was left freezing in the cold. Is this racism or what?! "

Sheku Syl Kamara, 22, Sierra Leone

Painting by Donna McCullough, USA

Colours

The colour of my face or my race
Red, yellow, black or blue
All these appearances
Should cause no interferences
It really shouldn't matter to you.

Religion or my age
Shouldn't cause a rage
Education, gender or ability
Or even my financial stability
It really shouldn't matter to you.

Equality and justice
Listen to us and trust us
To make the world peaceful
and fair;
Down with discrimination
We all must care
It all should matter to you!

Emily Mackinnon, USA

Racism against gypsies in the Czech Republic

66 *Like most countries, we too have to cope with racism and the hatred that goes with it. In the Czech Republic, there is a problem with gypsies. They consider themselves to be different from the majority of the people and are determined to live as they want to.*

The 'skinheads' believe that the gypsies are wasters and thieves. They want the gypsies to be made to leave the country. Others think that the only good gypsy is a dead one and that they should all be hanged. Violence between these groups is on the increase; people are getting injured and even killed. Something must be done to help them understand each other. I think that racist movements should be banned, but on the other hand, the gypsies make things worse for themselves by refusing to communicate with others. 99

Dan Kefer, 13, Czech Republic

ARTICLE

2

MADE SIMPLE

The same, but different

'Unity' by Monika Zouzelkova, 10,
Czech Republic

Caste system

66 *I am from Kathmandu, Nepal, and I belong to the Newari caste. A caste is a social group given to a person at birth. People from the lower castes are completely segregated from those in the higher castes. In city areas, the caste system is becoming less important, but it has not been eliminated completely. It is more difficult to fight the caste system in the villages, where people in the higher castes do not allow people from the lower castes to enter their houses, handle their food and water, or even to touch them. The system encourages the exploitation of the lower castes by the upper castes. This is one of the most blatant violations of human rights and it hampers the development of my country.* 99

Urjana Shrestha, 18, Nepal

Sexual orientation

We discovered that in many countries, lesbians and gays are still discriminated against because of their sexuality. This discrimination can vary from name-calling to being beaten up. Elsewhere, attitudes have changed a lot since the end of the 19th century, when Oscar Wilde, the well-known British writer, was sent to prison for having a relationship with a younger man. There are many pressure groups and campaigns trying to change public opinion.

The Paralympics

The first Paralympics were held in Rome in 1960, at a time when disabled people endured a great deal of discrimination. Although disabled people still face discrimination, the Paralympics has done an enormous amount to make people aware that disabled people are able to reach the very heights of human endeavour. The Paralympics, held alongside the Olympics every four years, are all about equality and inclusion. The games help to dispel the stigma surrounding disabled people and give acknowledgement to these elite athletes.

The world of women

Did you know that 8 March is Women's Day?

It's celebrated all over the world and marks the day in 1908 when women workers were burned to death in a factory in New York as they fought to improve working conditions.

Since then, the 20th century has seen a huge advancement in the status of women, who used to be forbidden from voting and owning property. In the 1960s the Feminist movement made men and women aware of sexual inequality. Women from all corners of the globe stood up for their rights as equal citizens. Now we see women in parliament as politicians and prime ministers. It is acceptable for women to become judges, soldiers and pilots. In fact, girls who receive the same standard of education as boys do far better in school, and in areas where women are educated the standard of living rises – so everyone benefits!

Unfortunately, there is still a lot to do! On the next two pages, you can read of abuses against women, some of which have thankfully been overcome. We have come a long way, but need to travel even further.

Illustration by
Sanid Zuko, 18,
Bosnia-Herzegovina

ARTICLE
2
MADE SIMPLE

Women's struggles

Women and money: the Grameen Bank

We think financial independence for women is extremely important. Although many women run households, it can be very difficult for them to start up their own businesses or get paid properly for their work. Why is this? Well, it's because they often don't earn enough and so banks won't give them loans. The Grameen Bank from Bangladesh sets out to try to solve this problem by giving women credit. The bank lends money to groups of women so that when one member of the group repays her loan, the next woman in the group receives hers. This means that the women all work together to make sure that their businesses succeed. Each year the bank gives out about four million loans to women in more than 35,000 villages in Bangladesh. Its work has given women the financial freedom they could have only dreamt of 20 years ago.

Female genital mutilation

In many African countries, men won't marry an uncircumcised girl, so the custom continues. Female circumcision is a barbaric practice still carried out today with crude tools on young girls between the ages of 4 and 13. The girls often bleed to death.

" *I was circumcised when I was four. I hate it and I don't want my daughter to be circumcised. I see no point to the painful mutilation that I have suffered and I feel that my family members abused my rights.* "

Kumba Ndure, 19, Gambia

Sati in India

Lots of people from India wanted to tell us about the cruel practice of sati, which took place up until the mid-19th century, where a widow was forced to be burned with her husband's body. This is such a dreadful and powerful image of the ultimate sacrifice of a woman. Here is one story. A woman got married, but her husband died within a few months. She was still weeping when she was suddenly asked to get ready to be made a sati. She cried for mercy but nobody listened to her. She was taken to the funeral with her dead husband. Hymns were chanted – she was treated as a goddess. She was made to sit with her husband on the wooden pyre, and burned alive. Many people campaigned to make sati illegal, which it now is – a true sign of women's struggles overcome.

Illustration by Jantien Roozenburg, 15, The Netherlands

A letter from Afghanistan

In Afghanistan, the Taliban, the military and political force that controls most of the country, states that girls shouldn't go to school and women can't have jobs. Below is a letter based on one that we were sent by a young girl who wishes to remain anonymous.

Dear Esther,

You said you wanted to know more about my life. Well, I can tell you because I have a lot of time to spare – too much time! I am now sitting at home as a virtual prisoner. The doors of the girls' school are shut so we can't get educated. It's as if darkness has cast a shadow over most of Afghan society, and especially on girls and women. This darkness is a regime that calls itself Islamic Taliban. The Taliban rulers have little or no education and justify all their actions by saying that they are following the words of the Koran.

So we cannot go to school and we can't go outside, even to the shops, unless we are dressed in a 'tent' and are accompanied by a male member of our family. We must wear slippers, not high-heeled shoes, so that no one will hear us. The sound of our feet is considered offensive to the ears of men. Women are not allowed to work and therefore have no say in social affairs or the way society is run. We sit at home like birds in a cage.

The Taliban says that women cannot work and girls cannot go to school, but there is nothing in the Koran which says this! The Taliban rulers do not understand what human rights are and have no respect for them. Now that all the rights of the Afghan have been trampled on at a national and international level we must take action. Other countries follow the laws of Islam but do not discriminate against their people in this way. Please hear our voices! Oh God, why doesn't the sun shine on the dark world of women and girls?

Anonymous

'Taliban Women' by
Arshak Sarkissian, 16, Armenia

The right to life

Everyone has the right to life, liberty and personal security.

When we sat down to write these pages, we soon found out that many of the editors had very different opinions about issues concerning the right to life. Some were for abortion and some were against. Some felt that the death penalty was necessary and others were passionately opposed. However, there was one thing that we all agreed on – that genocide is completely wrong and that if we could make the rules on this planet, one of our first laws would be to ban it. What do you think?

For and against abortion

> *The right to live is the most important in our world, and for that reason we must fight against abortion.*
> Alberto Granada, 17,
> Colombia

> *A woman who wants to have an abortion runs the risk of losing her life. She wants to kill a small child that has just begun to live.*
> Ali Chang, 19,
> Malaysia

> *Is it fair for a woman to have a child that she doesn't want? If a woman gets raped and becomes pregnant, is it fair for her to have a child who will remind her of that horror?*
> Jantien Roozenburg, 15,
> The Netherlands

> *You should be able to choose whether you have an abortion or not. You are the only one who can decide.*
> Natalia Ramirez, 12,
> Argentina

Illustration by Sanid Zuko,
18, Bosnia-Herzegovina

Genocide – murdering an entire race

Throughout history, there have been attempts by one people to systematically wipe out another. This is called 'genocide'. From the killing of indigenous peoples in the Americas, the Caribbean and Australasia to the Nazi death-camps to exterminate the Jews during the Second World War, the desire to completely destroy one's neighbours rears its ugly head again and again. In 1915 more than a million Armenians were massacred by the Turks. You might think that such massacres are a thing of the past, but in recent years, the international community sat back and watched while Hutus slaughtered whole Tutsi villages in Rwanda. There is no reason or logic in killing innocent people yet it goes on and on. It's important we don't forget this or the rest of our rights become irrelevant. How can we, as a global community, let this continue into our future? Remember that there is always a possible peaceful solution to conflict.

For and against the death penalty

I am against the death penalty because we as human beings have no right to take the life of the killer.
Toyin Ajasa-Oluwa, 15, UK

Suppose a thief enters your house, steals all your property and kills your only sister. Do you think he should be imprisoned or face the death penalty?
Vladimir Popov, 14, Russia

What happens if you make a mistake? It would be terrible if you killed someone who was innocent.
Alexander Woollcombe, 17, UK

The death penalty acts as a deterrent. If people know that they will die if they kill someone, it will make them think twice before doing it.
Brian Peterson, 13, Australia

Slavery – past and present

ARTICLE
4
MADE SIMPLE

No one shall be held in slavery. Slavery and the slave trade shall be completely forbidden.

In history books, the word 'slavery' appears all too often. Again and again, one group, people or race has appointed itself master of another. During Africa's colonial period, hundreds of thousands of Africans were turned into slaves and taken to the Americas. The European slave-drivers scarcely considered their African captives to be human at all. They beat them, chained them and humiliated them until the slaves lost their identity. Many died of illnesses and malnutrition before they reached their destination. In western Africa, much of the slave trade was organized by the African kings, who exchanged slaves for gunpowder and whisky.

William Wilberforce was one of the leaders in the fight to abolish slavery in the British Empire. Shortly after his death, in 1833, the Slavery Abolition Act was passed in the British Parliament, which helped put an end to this horror. Unfortunately, slavery still exists today in many different forms, from child-slavery to enforced prostitution. In some societies slavery has become so commonplace that there is little awareness that what is happening is wrong. It is time to fight against modern-day slavery, now!

Slavery on your doorstep!

Perhaps you think slavery is something that happens somewhere else – over there! In fact, in your nearest big city, there might be a young woman from the Philippines who finds herself working a 16–20-hour day, seven days a week with no holidays. Kalayaan is a European group that stands up for the rights of these workers and helps them to escape from their employers. Often distressed workers arrive at their offices with no passport, money or possessions!

Painting by
Arshak Sarkissian,
16, Armenia

26

Child camel jockeys

Imagine you are a poor Mauritanian or Indian six year-old boy whose parents have sold you for much-needed income. Then you are smuggled out of the country to the United Arab Emirates. You are crammed with other children into a small room and fed very little to keep you as light as possible. You are now a camel jockey. Below, a real young camel jockey tells us of his experiences.

66 *They took us and attached us with cords to the camels' backs. Those who refused or who were scared were beaten and forced on the camels. We were very frightened of falling off and dying. Children who fell could be trampled on by the camels. When we got too big to be jockeys, we were returned to our countries, but many of us had forgotten where our homes and parents were.* **99**

Anonymous

Iqbal Masih

Iqbal Masih is a brave hero who risked everything and spoke out against the cruel practice of forcing children into 'bonded labour'. This is when a child is sold to an employer in exchange for a loan of money to his or her parents. Iqbal was enslaved at a carpet loom from the age of four until the age of ten, when he escaped with the support of Pakistan's Bonded Labour Liberation Front (BLLF).

Iqbal received a special Reebok prize in December 1994 for his brave heart and hard work – he said he was "no longer afraid" of the carpet manufacturer who had owned him. Then, while he was cycling with two relatives in Pakistan, he was shot dead – nobody knows who the killer was. But the publicity his story received has made sure that many kids like him in the world, who are kept behind locked doors, are never, ever going to be forgotten.

Child prostitution

We heard many stories of young teenagers, mostly girls, but some boys, who had been forced into prostitution. The majority were poor or had come from broken homes. They all needed money which was vital to their survival. Lots of girls thought that they were getting jobs as waitresses, but as soon as they arrived their employers forced them to become prostitutes. They hoped that one day, when they had earned enough, they could escape their sickening life, but often this has proved impossible.

27

Torture: a living hell

ARTICLE **5** MADE SIMPLE

No one shall be tortured or given cruel, inhuman or degrading punishments.

Torture is one of the most upsetting of all human rights' abuses. Amnesty International reports that half of the world's governments torture their prisoners. How and why does this still go on? One thing is for sure, torture victims never forget. Many of them are unable to lead normal lives because their souls have been almost destroyed. We found out from the stories sent in that torture does not only exist during times of war, it is also common in the classroom and at home. Bullying, child abuse and family violence are all forms of torture and we must do all we can to stamp them out.

Lick the floor

"*My friend was the smallest boy in the first class. There was a stronger boy who used to bully him every day. He took my friend's lunch and ate it. Then he said, "Kneel down and lick the floor". My friend was crying but he started to lick the floor, because the strong boy was shouting at him. The other pupils were laughing. But why? Were they too small or too young? And why was the strong boy so bad? He wasn't hungry. Why did he want to do that? Was it hatred, envy or what?*"

Anonymous, Czech Republic

Picture by Peter Thompson, 17, UK

The Medical Foundation for the Care of Victims of Torture

Victims of torture often find it difficult to make friends and to like themselves. So when Helen Bamber from the UK visited Auschwitz, a Nazi concentration camp in Poland, and met former prisoners, she decided to set up a foundation to look after torture victims.

Her foundation originally helped survivors of camps such as Auschwitz, but in the past ten years it has helped 10,000 people from 70 countries. A team of doctors and therapists provides victims of violence with medical and social care, practical help and therapy. Their work has done much to make people world-wide aware of the problems associated with torture.

I'm a person, just like you

Everyone, everywhere has the right to be recognized as a person by the law.

In the mid-19th century, a slave ship called the Amistad landed in America and became the subject of a famous trial – were the African slaves on board 'people' or 'property'? Eventually, the American Supreme Court decided that they were people in their own right. Here are two more stories about people fighting for the rights everyone deserves.

Civil rights in the USA

In 1955, Rosa Parks, a black passenger on a city bus, refused to give up her seat for a white person. She believed that she had as much right as the whites to sit down. She was arrested and this sparked off a protest called the Montgomery boycott, when many blacks and whites refused to use the buses.

One man in particular realized that the time had come to take action and to fight for civil rights. Martin Luther King was a tireless civil-rights campaigner, but he absolutely insisted that all protest should be without violence. In 1963, he took part in a non-violent march to Washington DC, where he said the following famous words: "I have a dream that my four little children will one day live in a nation where they will not be judged by the colour of their skin, but by the content of their character." These struggles led to new laws recognizing the civil rights of African Americans.

Civil-rights campaigners paraded the streets with signs that said 'I am a man' so that the government would give them equal rights.

Apartheid

South Africa has been dominated by white people for around 300 years. In 1948 the ruling party decided on a policy of forced segregation or 'apartheid'. The whites in power thought they were racially superior to the blacks. This meant that black and white people were not allowed to live together, get married or be friends. There were special bus stops, lavatories and beaches for each race. The whites enjoyed the riches of the country, while the local people lived in virtual poverty.

The anti-apartheid movement stood up to this storm of discrimination. Many activists were killed or imprisoned, but world-wide, the movement gained strength. A boycott was organized, banning South Africa from trading and stopping them from taking part in international sporting events.

Eventually, apartheid fell. We must remember that it was the commitment of many people standing up to abuses of human rights that led to its demise. It proves that change is possible.

Painting by Arshak Sarkissian, 16, Armenia

We are all protected by law

Everyone is equal before the law and has the right to be protected equally by the law. We are all further protected by the law against any attempt to discriminate or to encourage others to discriminate amongst us.

Amnesty International reports that half of the world's governments jail people because of their beliefs, race, gender or ethnic origin. At trial, you should be treated fairly no matter who you are.

Nelson Mandela and 'New' South Africa

In 1994, to world-wide joy and happiness, Nelson Mandela became the first black president of South Africa. After 28 years in prison for his fight against apartheid, Mandela was released in 1990 and was asked by F.W. de Klerk, the then president, to help put an end to this terrible period in the country's history. Their dedicated work enabled South Africa to start afresh and for this they were both awarded the Nobel Peace Prize. In historic scenes, they organized free and fair elections and for the first time the black people of South Africa were able to choose their own government.

South Africa now has a Bill of Rights so that everyone is equal before the law and equally protected by the law. It is thanks to people like Nelson Mandela that such a change came about – he is a real human-rights hero.

Painting by Aminu Seidu, Ghana

Some tribes are more equal than others

We see no reason why some tribes should be better protected by the law than others. This report presents the opinion of a student, who wants to remain anonymous, on the escalating problems of tribalism in Kenya. He says that the ruling tribes are given better treatment than the others. The president is from the Kalenjin tribe and they receive the most privileges. In 1992, there were tribal clashes in Kenya which left 2,000 people dead and many others injured and homeless. People from the Kalenjin tribe were given arrows and guns by high-ranking government officials to fight other tribes. The non-Kalenjinis were arrested and locked up, while their enemies went free.

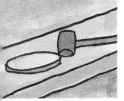

Fair treatment by fair courts

ARTICLE

8

MADE SIMPLE

If our rights are violated, we all have the right to take those who violate them to court and receive a fair judgement.

In many countries, people disappear daily. They are kidnapped, murdered, tortured... who knows what happens to them? No one! When this happens, people should be able to ask for legal help, but that's not always the case. Here is an example of one of the organizations that fights to help people find out where their missing relatives are.

Grandmothers of the 'disappeared'

Marina Mansilla, 15, from Argentina heard about the many people who went missing during the military dictatorship in Argentina in the 1970s. She went to visit 'Las Abuelas de la Plaza de Mayo' to find out the truth. 'Las Abuelas', a famous Argentinian organization, has been working to find the real identity of the 300 or so children who were kidnapped under the regime. At the time, thousands of people who disagreed with the regime were put in concentration camps and killed. Children who were born in these camps were taken away from their mothers and given to couples who were sympathetic to the dictatorship. Over the last 20 years, 'Las Abuelas' has found around 60 stolen young people, 33 of whom are now with their real families. Another 13 are with good foster parents and in contact with their biological families.

'Las Abuelas' has been frustrated at every turn by the authorities, who refuse to assist them in their search. They have tried to find out who is responsible for this wrong-doing but have met with a wall of silence. They would like to take the case to court to find out the truth but so far have not succeeded.

'Missing children': mothers and grandmothers parade the streets of Argentina, demanding that the government does more to help them in the quest to find their missing children.

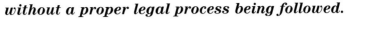

I've done **nothing** wrong!

ARTICLE **9** MADE SIMPLE

No one shall be arrested arbitrarily on a whim or held in prison, or forced into exile without a proper legal process being followed.

Picture by Aminu Seidu, 18, Ghana

Just imagine the confusion and fear of being accused of something you haven't done.

❝ *I was dragged out of the bus by four armed policemen to a waiting police van. I was thrown in a room for four days without my family's knowledge. I was terrified.* ❞
Anonymous, Kenya

Ugandan Asians in exile
The injustices suffered by Ugandan Asians are thankfully now over. We found out about their problems of the past.

Asians were brought to Uganda to build a railway in the late 19th century. They settled there and opened businesses. In 1908, they played an important role in constructing Uganda's capital city.

But when Major General Idi Amin Dada seized power in 1971, there was hostility towards Ugandan Asians over economic interests. A year later Amin gave the Asians 90 hours to leave the country. They were forced to leave their land and belongings behind. Amin gave their properties to his supporters. It was a terrible period. Then in 1991, the government of President Yoweri Museveni signed a treaty with the Asians, who returned and regained some of their property.

Fair trials

ARTICLE 10 MADE SIMPLE

Everyone charged with a crime, whatever their background, is entitled to an open and fair trial by an impartial court.

People don't always get fair trials – if you look closely you can find examples of this in almost any country. The law should ensure that all people are treated alike.

Ken Saro-Wiwa – injustice in Nigeria

Ken Saro-Wiwa's fight to stand up for what he believed in led to his imprisonment without a fair trial and ultimately his execution in 1995. We contacted his son, Ken Wiwa, to tell us what happened.

"My father helped form the Movement for the Survival of the Ogoni People (MOSOP), an organization whose aim was to help the Ogoni people organize themselves in the peaceful defence of their lands and culture.

On 3 January 1993, 300,000 Ogonis came surging out of their villages in support of MOSOP and the Ogoni Bill of Rights. This set down demands for a clean environment and the right to a fair share of the resources being taken from us. That day, now called Ogoni Day, marked a change of attitude among the people. My father said: 'If I had died today, I would have died a happy man.' Less than three years later, he was dead.

He was arrested in May 1995 and charged with murder. After a long show trial, widely condemned by many world leaders, he was

Ken Saro-Wiwa

sentenced to death and hanged. Very few people doubt that my father was framed. His real crime was to draw attention to corporate greed and the human rights' abuses of a regime which has pillaged a people's resources without putting anything back. He used his mental capacity to challenge his oppressors, who reacted the only way they know – with violence. Although he is dead, my father has made his point. People like you reading this article now know who the Ogoni are and what they stand for."

Innocent until proven guilty

Everyone charged with a crime has the right to be presumed innocent until proven guilty.

Everyone should be given a fair chance. It is often difficult to work out who did what at the scene of a crime, and police everywhere make mistakes. Sometimes the people who are arrested haven't done anything wrong, so it is vital that they aren't badly treated or harassed before they are convicted. This is particularly important when you think about the effect that TV, newspapers and the Internet can have on what we think. There have been several cases recently where the public has hounded famous people accused of committing crimes before they have got anywhere near a courtroom. The media report only one version of a story, which isn't necessarily correct.

Picture by
Arshak Sarkissian,
16, Armenia

I am innocent until proven guilty

The policemen came to arrest me,
They locked me up,
Thrown into a small room without any light,
Although I had done nothing.
I did not know what I was charged with.
The day after, they interrogated me.
I understand it was about a robbery,
Unfortunately, my honesty made them furious.

They needed a guilty person to close the file,
And I was about to become the scapegoat.
They ordered me to get undressed,
Then they started the harsh treatment.
They whipped me, kicked me and beat me,
For three days, they used all ways and means
To try to get a confession from me.

At one moment I wanted to give up,
Sacrifice my freedom to be left in peace.
They dishonoured me, tortured me,
I could not distinguish days from nights.
On the eighth day, I was released
and the guilty arrested.
Today, I still live with the memories.
I suffered; I cannot forget.

Karim Boubred, 20, Algeria

The influence of the media

At the 1997 Atlanta Olympics, a security guard called Richard Jewell spotted a backpack moments before the bomb inside it exploded. At first, he was hailed a hero but then an article appeared in the Atlanta Journal headlined "FBI suspects 'hero guard' may have planted bomb". After that, he was hounded by TV and newspaper reporters who described him as a sort of weirdo with an unstable history. As a result of the coverage, a large percentage of the US public thought him guilty. Later, federal officials cleared him of any involvement whatsoever, but Jewell says his "name is ruined forever". The media do not always know all the facts.

The right to **privacy**

ARTICLE
12
MADE SIMPLE

Everyone has the right to be protected from arbitrary interference of their privacy, whether it be unfounded attacks on their reputation or interference in their home, family or personal letters.

Privacy means that your business is your business – you should be able to live your life without being pestered or spied on. Daniel, our editor from Cameroon, says that in many boarding schools in his country, all letters to pupils are routinely read first by the teachers. Often prisoners have their mail opened and checked, to stop them from planning escapes. Also, in many countries, human-rights activists and government opponents have their telephones bugged and their movements closely monitored. Is there ever a time when it is right to invade someone's privacy? What do you think?

'Who's watching who?!?'
by Sanid Zuko, 18,
Bosnia-Herzegovina

Freedom of the press

Since the death of Diana, Princess of Wales, there has been much discussion about people's privacy. Lorena Lara, 16, from Argentina wrote to us about her concerns. "There doesn't seem to be any kind of limit to privacy, when it comes to obtaining the best story. Just look at the Royal Family in the UK.

Love scandals, fake videos and even the dreadful death of Princess Diana helped to sell huge numbers of magazines and books." What do you think? Should the press have freedom to print what they like? What about famous people? They often seek publicity, but should the press be allowed to take photos of them wherever they go?

Freedom to move!

ARTICLE

13

MADE SIMPLE

Everyone is free to move about their country and live where they like within it. Everyone has the right to come and go from their country as they like.

In 1991, the fall of the Iron Curtain meant that millions of people could do what they had dreamed of doing for most of their lives. They could travel. In Berlin, there was an enormous celebration and thousands came together to tear down the wall that had divided their city for so long. For many, the Berlin Wall had come to symbolize a barrier to their freedoms – and with its destruction, Germany became free once more.

Most people take for granted the fact that they can travel or live anywhere they like in their own country, but in some countries this basic human right is still not respected. We researched the following stories about Cyprus and North Korea.

Picture by Arshak Sarkissian, 16, Armenia

Cyprus

Ever since 1974, there has been no freedom of movement between north and south on the island of Cyprus. Turkish Cypriots live in the north and Greek Cypriots live in the south. Most young Cypriots have never met anyone from 'the other side'. The 'Green Line' is the barricade that divides the capital, Nicosia, in two. Constantina Georgiou, 19, says, "We listen to the same songs, we watch the same movies, we love the same land – it's about time they stopped treating us as different."

North Korea

In The Democratic People's Republic of Korea (North Korea), people need special permission to travel outside their own villages. Sometimes this takes so long to come through that they are not able to make the trip. The government also strictly controls permission to live in, or even to enter, the city of Pyongyang. The only people who are allowed to leave the country are officials and certain favoured artistes, academics or athletes.

The right to **asylum**

ARTICLE
14
MADE SIMPLE

Everyone has the right to seek and to enjoy asylum in other countries from persecution, except when they are charged with genuinely non-political crimes like robbery or murder, or anything else in conflict with the spirit of the United Nations.

Imagine being persecuted, being forced out of your home, leaving all your favourite possessions, not knowing if you might see your home again. It's a terrifying thought. But that's not the end of it. Imagine trying to get asylum. Imagine arriving in a foreign country, where nobody cares about you, where you have no money, no friends, where you can't speak the language and have no idea what will happen to you tomorrow. And even when you get permission to stay, you have to rebuild your life. Unfortunately, there are about 30 million refugees in the world – twice as many as there were in 1985! When you next meet a refugee, think about what they have been through to get there.

Equal chance

Refugees are normal.
They are no different
from anyone else.
They should be treated
normally and equally.
Racism against refugees must stop.

Everyone has
an equal right to education.
Because of language problems
and what they have been through,
refugees should receive special help
to give them an equal chance.
This help should be
fair and equal for all refugees.

It should not separate or divide
refugees from other students.
All support for refugees should aim
to make them feel
a normal part of the class,
where everyone has an equal
chance and is treated
fairly and equally.

Refugees are normal.
Refugees are welcome here.
We're all different,
but we're all equal.

Pupils from George Mitchell School, UK, wrote this poem together to raise awareness about refugees.

Illustration submitted by the Human Rights Education Programme, Pakistan

Here are some fictional diary entries, based on the real-life experiences of a young Kurdish refugee who had to flee from Turkey.

September 4th 1997

Dear Diary,

Today my father was killed in the market-place before my eyes. The soldiers shot him three times in the chest, and he died instantly...

There was nothing that I could do but cry – my father was dead...

September 7th 1997

Dear Diary,

The soldiers came to the house and I had to hide. Never in my life have I felt so much fear. I crouched in a small cupboard under the stairs for two hours until they left. Many of my neighbours and friends were killed. I realized that I had to leave this country before something terrible happened to me.

September 10th 1997

Dear Diary,

I left with very little luggage because I didn't want the soldiers to know I was going. When I arrived at the airport it was very noisy, and as I boarded the flight, I knew I was finally free.

September 11th 1997

Dear Diary,

When I got off the plane, I was told to go into a small waiting room full of people. The sign above the door said 'Detention Centre waiting room'. I waited in the room for two hours, then suddenly my name was called. I was taken into another small waiting room, where I was asked questions about why I left my country. Finally I was driven by van to a massive building signed 'DETENTION CENTRE'... I had no idea that it would be like this... my troubles were just beginning...

The right to a **nationality**

Everyone has the right to a nationality. No one shall be arbitrarily deprived of their nationality nor denied the right to change their nationality should they wish to do so.

A dictionary definition of nationality is "a people who live in the same place, speak the same language and have their history". In other words, to have a nationality means to have your own state. But there is much more to nationality than just this. It means a certain way of life, with your own festivals, family trees, a national anthem and special native costumes to wear. Nationality allows you to have your own passport, currency and proper frontiers.

Nationality also means simple things, like taking part in the Olympics or laughing at the same jokes. This helps you to know who you are and makes you feel like you belong. Many wars happen because one government imposes its will over another and keeps its people under control by forcing them to live without rights. This wouldn't happen if people accepted that no nation is better than another. People should be able to choose their government.

Kosovo

One of the members of our editorial committee comes from Kosovo, a troubled province of ex-Yugoslavia. She gave us the following report.

In 1989, Kosovo lost its autonomy. Kosovo Albanians make up 90% of the population, yet they are now governed by the 10% of Serbs from the Serbian capital, Belgrade. Albanians lost the right to retain their language and culture, and to choose their own government. They tried to write their own fate by voting for independence in the Kosovo Referendum of 1991, but the Serbs didn't agree to it.

Over the last ten years, Albanians have formed a parallel system of schools, government and funding. They tried to keep out of the Bosnian war by resisting peacefully. But after the massacre of children and old people in Drenica by Serb soldiers, the villagers took up arms to defend themselves. Diplomatic negotiations have broken down, and many say they will now fight until they win their independence.

Young Kosovo Albanians on a march protest for the right to have their own country.

Unrepresented Nations and Peoples Organization

Unrepresented Nations and Peoples Organization (UNPO) was created by nations and peoples who are not represented in organizations like the UN. Founded in 1991, UNPO has 50 member organizations representing over 100 million people denied their nationality. They are struggling to regain their lost countries, to preserve their cultural identities, to protect their basic human and economic rights and to safeguard the natural environment.

The following groups belong UNPO:

- Abkhazia ● Assyria ● Aboriginals of Australia ● Acheh/Summatra ● Albanians in Macedonia
- Bashkortostan ● Batwa ● Bougainville ● Buryatia ● Cabinda ● Chechen Republic
- Chittagong Hill Tracts ● Circassians ● East Timor ● Eastern Turkestan ● Hawaii ● Ingushetia
- Inkeri ● Iraqi Turkman ● Karenni ● Kumyk ● Kurdistan ● Mapuche ● Mon ● Nagaland
- Ogoni ● Scania ● Shan State ● Taiwan ● Tatarstan ● Tibet ● West Papua ● Zanzibar

An unrepresented person appeals to her oppressor

I look at myself in the mirror,
I don't like what I see.
But there's no way I'm going to stop knocking
On all those walls built in front of me.

I don't want to whine,
I don't want to make you cry,
I just want to make you care,
I just want to make you try.

What is it exactly that you mind about me?
Is it the language that I speak?
Is it the colour of my blood?
Is it the purity of my heart?
or maybe you mind ME in OUR part.

I'm not a marionette for them to play with,
I want to burn these ropes that hurt so much.
Stop reminding me that I'm not allowed to,
Stop forbidding my education,
Stop ignoring my self-determination.

Stop making me flee,
I'm not here to fight:
I'm here to stop fighting
Because I've seen it on TV,
That war is the worst way to get free.

Jeta Xharra, 20, Kosovo

'Flags' by Gözde Boğa, 15, Turkey

The Universal Declaration of Human Rights
Part Two

Economic, social and cultural rights
The basic right to freedom and equality

Opposite: drawing anonymous, UK

Marriage and family

ARTICLE
16
MADE SIMPLE

At 16, or an agreed legal age, any man or woman, whatever their race, nationality or religion, may marry and found a family. The man and the woman have equal rights both during the marriage and if they get divorced. No one shall be forced into a marriage against their will. The family is the basic building block of all societies and shall be protected by the law.

Are you looking forward to getting married? Lots of women aren't because they won't have a say in when they will marry, whom they will marry, when they will have children or how large their family will be. Many countries have granted women equal rights with men in matters of marriage, divorce and family property. But in some places, girls marry when they are still children. These 'child brides' have limited opportunities in life and are often stuck in a web of poverty. Marriage agreements should be based on mutual respect and freedom of choice.

Multiple marriages

Do you think it's wrong to have more than one wife? What if you could have more than one husband? Polygamy, which means having more than one wife, is common among Uganda's Ankole people. When a man takes another wife, he often doesn't have the means to support more than one family. This leads to neglect of wives and children, and quarrelling and unhappiness in the home!

Illustration by Zuzana Zuzna, 11, Czech Republic

Girls betrothed in infancy

We were really surprised at the way different cultures view marriage. It was hard to believe news from the Macedonian organization, 'The First Children's Embassy in the World', that some European girls are betrothed in infancy. It happens among Macedonian Muslims in a village called Labuniste. On the radio there, you hear musical messages of congratulations from relatives for the marriage of children only a few months old. It is certainly not a case of 'marriage being entered into only with the free and full consent of the intending spouses'. The custom has been observed for generations and no one will break the tradition.

66 *One of the biggest evils in Indian society is the 'dowry system'. This means that if the bride does not bring any dowry from her parents' house, the bride is harassed, tortured and sometimes burnt alive. It is high time we got rid of the evil practice of dowry taking. Boys should refuse to take a dowry and girls should firmly say no to greedy bridegrooms. Thus, the evil system would be put to an end. SAY NO TO DOWRY.* **99**

Surabhi Maru, India

66 *In Uganda, forced marriage can take place. A man comes and he says, "Give me your daughter and I'll give you five cows." The father agrees and the man takes the girl.* **99**

Sarah Nalubwama, Uganda

66 *Marriage is associated with happiness and responsibility, and it's a symbol of maturity. The issue of forced marriage does not exist in our society and once a couple gets married, we hope they live a happy life with their kids. Marriage is one of the greatest things in life: staying with your wife and kids and planning things together for the future, rather than hanging out in a bar with other girls like some boys I know! That's all I want!!!* **99**

Alfred Syl Kamara, 15, Sierra Leone

What's happened **to my home?**

ARTICLE
17
MADE SIMPLE

Everyone is entitled to own things, whether on their own, or as a group or family. No one shall be arbitrarily deprived of their property.

Imagine how you would feel if your family had lived in one place for centuries, yet someone came along and claimed your home as theirs. You wouldn't like it! We've heard and read about many people whose property has been taken away from them. We found that there is never a 'true' version of a historical event because there is always the slant of the person writing it. Here are some of our perspectives.

Indigenous people – a history of shame

In the late 19th century, in the Canadian province of Alberta, government officials negotiated with indigenous people to make them hand over their land. The officials persuaded the chiefs that they should pass on ownership of their land in return for money and tools. The indigenous people couldn't understand the languages of the Europeans and many of them handed over their properties, hoping that it was the best thing to do.

The Europeans, thinking that their race and culture was 'superior' to that of the local people, tried to force them to abandon their way of life and placed them in special segregated reserves. Today, the situation has improved and the government is trying to make amends for the past, but sadly, much of their culture has already been lost.

The Australian aboriginals

It was the same sort of story in Australia when the British colonized it in 1788. Using brute force, they captured and enslaved many aboriginals and killed thousands more. Wild land and desert areas were cultivated and mined. The aboriginals lost many of their sacred sites and could no longer live as they had done for centuries.

Nowadays, the whites and aboriginals live together, side by side, but the problems are still there. The land rights of the aboriginals remain very limited and raging disputes sour the relationships between the two groups. The nomadic tribes that once roamed freely across the great Australian deserts have been deprived of their homeland and way of life.

The Chiapas people in Mexico have had a raw deal!

In 1521, the Spanish conquered Mexico and destroyed the Aztec empire. Today, many of the indigenous people still live in a mountainous region in the south of Mexico, called Chiapas. Driven from their ancestral lands during the Spanish colonial period, many of the Chiapas people are now resettled in camps. However, they are still asking for their land to be returned. Because their requests have been ignored, frustration has turned to violence.

Meanwhile their land is being degraded by mining and logging companies.

Alejandro Jiminez from Mexico writes, "Most Mexican people believe that it's time to give the Chiapas people back what they have lost. So it's up to the Mexican government to put their words into action!"

And what about Palestine?

Both the Arabs and Israelis strongly believe that they have rights to the same land. Palestinian Arabs who had lived in their homes and villages for thousands of years saw them disappear when the state of Israel was created. The decision to form the state was taken in 1947 by the UN in New York – without consulting the Palestinians. Many people think that since then, Arab property rights have been consistently abused, but the Jewish Israelis think it's their homeland, too.

Picture by Sanid Zuko, 18, Bosnia-Herzegovina

Freedom of thought

ARTICLE

18

MADE SIMPLE

Everyone has the right to think and believe what they want, to change their mind if they want to, to pray or worship as they feel inclined, and to teach about, observe and organize religious festivals as they feel appropriate.

Think of all the people who have put forward ideas about how the world was created, or what happens after we die, or what is the best way to run a country. Who is right? How do we know? When you think about it like this, you soon realize that there's no right or wrong answer. Isn't it therefore wrong to persecute people for their beliefs? Isn't it wrong to stop someone from practising their religion? From the Christian crusades to the shooting of supporters of democracy in Tiananmen Square, China, people have suffered for what they believe. In Saudi Arabia, Christian church services are not allowed. In Northern Ireland, Catholics and Protestants are killed because of their religion. When will this end?

Ngawang Sangdrol: prisoner of conscience.

Would you be prepared to go to prison for your religion?

That's what a Tibetan nun, Ngawang Sangdrol, did in August 1990, when she was only 13 years old. She and other Buddhist nuns from the Garu monastery went to a demonstration calling for Tibetan independence. Ngawang was arrested and even though, at 13, she was too young to be tried, she was held prisoner for nine months.

On her release, Ngawang was forbidden to rejoin her monastery, but this didn't stop her from doing it. She was arrested again in 1992 for demonstrating, and sentenced to three years imprisonment. Whilst in prison, Ngawang and twelve other Buddhist nuns made secret tapes of uplifting Tibetan protest songs. She was given a further six years in prison! The Body Shop and Amnesty International have launched a campaign for her release.

Picture by Sanid Zuko,
18, Bosnia-Herzegovina

Archbishop Desmond Tutu: anti-apartheid hero

In preparation for this book, we gave the contributors the task of interviewing their human-rights heroes. Yolande van Rensburg and Bushra Razock from South Africa went to interview Archbishop Desmond Tutu to find out his ideas about religion and human rights. This is what he said:

"A country that has no religion would be an extremely weird country. We are created to be religious, and being religious really means being open to the mysterious, to the holy, to the good and to the beautiful. It would be a very, very sad day if there was no space for religion. I myself would say that South Africa should not claim to be a religious, Christian country. It should be a country that says it is secular, secular in the sense that the government does not try to impose one religious view on its people. We have a diversity of religions in our country and there should be a rule for all of them. Everyone can think whatever they want – everyone has the right to freedom of thought. We ought to make it possible for our country to respect other religions, and just to say that as a government we allow freedom of religion, which is a constitutional right."

Yolande van Rensburg and Bushra Razock with Archbishop Tutu.

Free to say what you want

Everyone is free to think and say what they want, without interference, in any media and in any country that they want.

"Oh, you can't do that." "Oh, you can't say that." How many times has somebody said that to you? If you're sitting there thinking that nobody has, then you are a very lucky person. Over the centuries, lots of people have been prevented from saying what they think. Artists and writers in particular have experienced this problem, as many controversial pictures and books have been burned. You might think that it's always wrong to destroy someone else's work, but think again. What do you feel about people who put pornography or racist literature on the Internet? Should they be allowed to do this or should they be banned? We mostly agree that everyone should have the right to say what they think, but it's not always straightforward!

A sound unheard
You hear me cry,
You hear me mutter.
But still it doesn't really matter.
I try to scream,
I try to speak,
But you still control my speech.
This determination in my voice;
This persistence to continue till I believe;
My right to freedom of speech.
Freedom of expression is my vision,
That one day we will no longer dream,
but live a successful fantasy.
Which is blinded in the clouds of reality.
Toyin Ajasa-Oluwa, 15, UK

Aung San Suu Kyi: Nobel Peace Prize Winner

Aung San Suu Kyi led her National League for Democracy Party to victory in elections in Burma in 1990. The results were ignored by the military government, who had earlier gunned down students campaigning for democracy in the capital, Rangoon. Ms Suu Kyi was placed under house arrest. Even though she sees little of her family or friends, she continues to fight for democracy. Her period of house arrest ended in 1995, but the military still watch her constantly and tap her phone. She is not allowed to meet with her supporters. She says, "The regaining of my freedom has in turn imposed a duty on me to work for the freedom of the other women and men who have suffered far more – and who continue to suffer far more – than I have." Why does she do this when she could get on a plane and leave? It's because of her passionate belief in freedom – freedom to say what she pleases and to protest against the tyranny of the military regime.

" When my family eats together in the evening, I'm not allowed to say anything. It's not because I don't have anything to say, it's because I'm the youngest. I often sit there and listen to the conversation and I want to say something, but I can't. Only my eldest brother is allowed to talk. Why can't I have the chance to talk? "
Richard Mbembe, 17, Nigeria

" Last week I read in the newspaper about someone who had been put in prison for saying something against his government. This is so wrong. Everyone should be able to think and say what they like, as long as they aren't lying. If you believe something from the bottom of your heart – say it and don't be afraid. "
Liam O'Neill, 13, Ireland

" It makes me so mad when people don't take me seriously. Just because I'm young doesn't mean I haven't got anything worthwhile to say. Not only should I have freedom of expression, I should also have the right to be listened to!!! "
Juan da Silva, 17, Peru

'Gagged' by Damien Boltauzer, 13, Canada

Meet where **you like**

ARTICLE
20
MADE SIMPLE

Everyone has the right to hold peaceful meetings and form associations, but no one shall be forced to join any association.

Meeting is one of the most important things we do. Meeting up with others enables us to share ideas, make decisions and plan our lives. Without meetings, how would we get anything done?! In some countries, people are prevented by the authorities from holding a meeting or forming an association. Why? What are the authorities afraid of? All you achieve by preventing meetings is discontent!

Students in South Korea

We have received reports from South Korean students who say that they are prevented by the police and the government from holding certain political meetings and organizing peaceful demonstrations. Many of them have been arrested because of their alleged association with North Korea. They would like to see a unified Korea, but they cannot form associations and often have their meetings disrupted. Yang Hyon Cha, a student who went to the World Youth Festival in Cuba in 1997, tells us she was arrested on her return because it was supposed that   she had been meeting with North Koreans.

Picture by Damien
Boltauzer, 13, Canada

Drawing by Michael
Heequaye, Ghana

52

Bhima Sangha

Here is a problem. In many countries, children work. Lots of people and governments agree that this must stop, but in the meantime we think that these children need employment rights. We heard about the Bhima Sangha, which is a union made up entirely of working children in India. They are not officially allowed to be a union and they face resistance from their employers and even their parents, but they still think it is important to meet. They want to protect their rights as workers now, but importantly, want to stop child labour in the future.

Artwork border by Urjana Shrestha, 18, Nepal

The children of the Bhima Sangha wrote and told us how the union started.

"In a small village lived a family. The children, Ravi and Radha, worked hard helping their parents and were domestic helps in other homes. They were very keen to go to school but they never had time.

As Ravi grew older he started working in the city. There he met Bhimanna, an activist involved in helping working children. Bhimanna said, 'I work with children like you. We will tell you how unions help children and we will also teach you certain life skills.'

Ravi was very happy and told his friend Girish the good news. They went to Bhimanna's union to find out more, and then decided to get together some working children. To begin with only a few children joined them. They encouraged more children to come by playing games for half an hour and then talking to them about their problems.

The children asked, 'What can we do about our problems?' Ravi said, 'If we want to find a solution to our problems, then we need to get together and build our own union – the Bhima Sangha. If we do this with determination, we can build a new world. Let this be our plan for the future.**"**

The right to **democracy**

ARTICLE
21
MADE SIMPLE

Everyone has the right to have a say in the government that rules them, through freely elected representatives. Regular elections in which everyone has the right to a free and secret vote shall be the only basis for the authority of a government and everyone shall have equal right to the public services that such governments provide.

Democracy may not work perfectly, but it is still the best form of government humans have come up with. If people are free to vote as they please, without being pressured or bribed, this ensures you get the system of government the majority wants. A good democracy makes public services, health and schooling available for everyone – not just for a privileged few. The good news is that however much you hear about corrupt leaders and dictatorships, they are greatly outnumbered by democratic governments.

'Right to vote' by Virginia Rivilli, Ariadna Silva, Carla Spagnolo, Paula Daveloza, all from Argentina

These are some of the countries that have become democratic in the last 20 years:

Argentina, Bosnia-Herzegovina, Brazil, Bulgaria, Central African Republic, Chile, Croatia, Czech Republic, Democratic Republic of Congo, East Germany, El Salvador, Estonia, Guatemala, Hungary, Lithuania, Latvia, Mozambique, Namibia, Nicaragua, Panama, Paraguay, Peru, Poland, Russia, Romania, Slovakia, Slovenia, South Africa, Uganda, Ukraine, Uruguay, Zimbabwe.

Democracy is precious

Democracy is hard to establish but easily destroyed. In Sierra Leone in 1992, democracy was destroyed in a single night by rebellious army officers. It took almost two years to re-establish. We should never take it for granted. All of us should use our right to vote.

Heroes of democracy

Since the signing of the Universal Declaration, there have been many heroes of democracy.

The President of the Czech Republic, Václav Havel, guided Czechoslovakia towards democracy in 1989. During Communist rule, he was imprisoned for his belief in the value of human rights.

Mahatma Gandhi was assassinated just before the Declaration was signed. He ensured that India became the world's biggest democracy by demanding that there be elections when India gained independence in 1947.

The United Nations is also a hero for the support it has given to governments trying to make their elections truly fair. Its hard work has helped to bring about democracy in Angola, Namibia, Mozambique, and many countries in eastern and central Europe.

Dictators – a rogues gallery

There are a lot of governments that pay lip-service to democracy but that are in fact dictatorships. Elections are 'rigged' and corrupt, while human rights are ignored. Over the years there have been notorious dictators in various countries around the world. Here are a few that we came up with.

Who? Adolf Hitler – Germany
When? 1933–1945
What? Hitler believed that the Germans were the 'master race'. He hated Jews, homosexuals, gypsies and anyone who refused to obey him. He sent millions of Jews to concentration camps.

Who? Pol Pot – Cambodia
When? 1975–1978
What? He was responsible for the 'killing fields', where one million out of a population of seven million were killed by execution or overwork. He killed people who wore glasses because he considered them to be intellectuals.

Who? Major General Idi Amin Dada – Uganda
When? 1971–1979
What? Thousands of people suffered under his cruel and crazy regime. People were thrown over cliffs, piles of skeletons were found by roadsides, and if any women were caught wearing slippers in the streets, they were made to eat them!

Who? General A. Pinochet Ugarte – Chile
When? 1973–1990
What? Pinochet is still commander-in-chief of the Chilean Army. Some 3,000 people disappeared or were killed during Pinochet's military dictatorship. There are those who think that Pinochet has helped the Chilean economy.

Illustrations by Sanid Zuko, 18, Bosnia-Herzegovina

The right to **social security**

Every member of a society has the right to a safety net that will provide the money and status necessary for them to enjoy a dignified life in their society. Individually and together, all nations shall struggle to provide that safety net for all people on earth.

'A world with healthcare and a world without' by Urjana Shrestha, 18, Nepal

Did you know that on average we are living much longer than we did 50 years ago – between 30 and 40 years longer in some cases? We are better fed, healthier, better educated, and we have more access to clean drinking water and less exposure to fatal diseases. The World Health Organization has eliminated the disease smallpox from the whole world. The last cases of polio and Guinea worm are now being eradicated. Cholera, diptheria, typhus and many other diseases that sent our ancestors to early graves are now almost gone.

Progress must continue

The percentages sound good, but the number of people living in absolute poverty, with no access to any kind of social security, has in fact risen. The UN and most western governments have pledged time and time again to eliminate poverty from our earth, and we know that it is possible – the amount of money required to succeed is equal to the collected wealth of the seven richest people on the planet. We all think it's just a matter of making a plan and putting it into action. We must fight to make it happen!

> *If you're a baby born in Gambia, the odds against your surviving are high because of poor delivery techniques, common infectious diseases and unclean water.*
> Kumba Ndure, 19, Gambia

> *In Kenya, two patients often have to share a bed, sleeping head to toe.*
> John Atwiambo, 17, Kenya

Illustration submitted
by the Human Rights
Education Programme,
Pakistan

Workers' rights

ARTICLE
23
MADE SIMPLE

Everyone has the right to work, to choose their job and to join a trade union. Everyone should have good working conditions, equal pay for equal work and unemployment benefit or income supplement if their pay does not ensure a decent standard of living.

There's one major problem here. If there are no jobs around, who can guarantee you the right to work? Similarly, in a poor country, how can the government pay everyone unemployment benefit and supplements if there is no money for basic health care? A government can make laws to ensure that men and women get equal pay for equal work, which is only fair. But it is more difficult to guarantee work. This is why we feel we need to become more creative about work. If jobs do not exist, we should see how we can build small businesses to meet the needs of the local community; businesses that are profitable but also eco-friendly and sustainable. Maybe also if there isn't enough work to go around we need to learn how to share it.

Child labour rights

This is an extremely difficult issue – should children have the right to work? In the UK, no child under 14 may work legally, even part-time. But in some developing countries, ten year-olds are the major bread-winners in a family! How can a global human right be written to cover the needs of all countries? Some people feel that child labour is so terrible that it should be stopped immediately. Others say that if you did this, life would become much worse for the families who depend on their children's wages. Somehow we have to find a way to make sure that all children have the opportunity to receive schooling. If all children had compulsory free education for at least part of the day, then they would have a chance to get a better job and climb out of the poverty trap in which they find themselves.

Illustrations submitted by the
Human Rights Education Programme, Pakistan

Equal pay for equal work

Do you think it's fair that in the USA in 1996, a white woman earned on average 73¢ for every dollar earned by a man, while an African-American woman earned an equivalent 65¢? Many women think it deeply unfair and participated in an Equal Pay Day, where 107 women's groups demonstrated together for equal pay. They have also introduced the Paycheck Fairness Act into the US Congress, which will force companies to pay equal amounts to men and women. Things are getting better: in 1965, a woman earned 60¢ for every dollar a man earned, so they've improved by 13¢ in 31 years!

Painting by Urjana Shrestha, 18, Nepal

Watchdog on trade-union rights!

Question: who watches over trade-union rights? Answer: the International Labour Organization (ILO), in Geneva, Switzerland. The ILO helps trade unions and workers to stop exploitation. Joining a trade union, which is an association that looks after the rights of workers, is often the only way that an individual can stand up to the might of a big company.

The ILO has set up a Commission of Inquiry to look at places where trade-union rights have been abused. Recently it has found problems in Colombia and Sudan, where trade-unionists are frequently imprisoned or 'disappear'.

The right to **play**

Everyone has the right to rest and leisure, and holidays from time to time.
No one shall be forced to work long and unreasonable hours.

Everybody needs time off. Otherwise, we would be absolutely exhausted. Many of us take this right for granted and for us, going shopping, going to the cinema, or playing sport is part of everyday life. Unfortunately, there are millions of people around the world who are unable to enjoy leisure time. Those in bonded labour are treated as slaves and are not allowed time to relax. In some societies, women can't leave the house and are forbidden from taking part in sport and other social activities. Disabled people, orphans and mentally handicapped people are locked away in some parts of the world. They deserve to live a fun and fulfilling life, too.

'The Right to Play' by Mia Rivera, 11,
Philippines

Too much work can kill

During our editorial meeting, we were visited by a professor from Korea, who told us about the education system in the Far East. She said that in many countries, such as South Korea and Japan, children don't get much time to play. A typical day starts at seven o'clock; they are at school by eight and work hard until four, with just 20 minutes' break for lunch. At home, two hours homework until seven, then out to private classes until ten.

After that, they fit in another hour of homework before bedtime. Many children are not allowed to watch TV or enjoy free-time. The professor told us, "Children who live in these countries don't know how to play, they don't know how to rest. This pressure is too much for a child. In fact, already there are stories of 16 year-olds who have committed suicide because they can't stand the pressure."

"I've got a holiday on the 15th of August, for me that is freedom."
Anonymous, Bhima Sangha, India

Illustration by Melina C. D'Auria, 15, Argentina

A bed and **some food**

ARTICLE **25** MADE SIMPLE

Everyone, especially mothers and children, has the right to a decent standard of living with appropriate housing, health care, food and social services in the event of unemployment, sickness, disability, widowhood, old age or other circumstances beyond his or her control.

Cairo, London, Nairobi, Istanbul, Bogotá, New York, Mexico City... the list goes on. What do they all have in common? Homelessness. Many of the victims living on the streets are children. Sometimes they have run away from home because they have suffered abuse. Often they are there because their families can't afford to feed them. Some of them beg, while others sell matches or flowers, or clean car windows. In Mexico City, many live on the outskirts and travel for an hour and a half to get to the fashionable Pink Zone, where they clean the windows of luxury cars for a couple of coins.

" *I want to go to school to learn things and to play with other kids. I wish I wasn't poor and I didn't have to work.* **"**

Guadalupe, 5, Mexico

'Homeless' by Georgina Barrows, 15, UK

" *I am a seventh grade, living in Pakistan. Even though I'm still young, I can see things that I know could be changed if someone cared. Poverty is a very big issue. Most of the population does not have proper homes; the poor make their houses from cloth and straw. Some people sleep and live on the sidewalk. I think maybe no one cares now, but perhaps my generation will care and make my country better for everyone, because everyone has a right to a home.* **"**

Naiha Ali, 13, Pakistan

Opposite: 'Boy in the Rubble' by Ruth Hardwicke, 16, UK

From the streets to university

"*I started living on the streets of Bogotá, Colombia, when I was only seven years old. I left home to live in the gutters because my family couldn't afford to feed me. Over three years, I learnt all about poverty and I saw firsthand the cruelty of Bogotá society.*

People hated us. At night, a drunk taxi driver would get angry and shoot at us. If a gang didn't like you, they would kill you. The police used to beat me and my friends frequently, just because we were living on the streets and begging for money. To survive on the streets there are just two laws: the law of strength and the law of silence.

When I went to sleep, I never knew whether I would wake up again. I knew the violence of the night in Bogotá, I saw the alcoholics, the homeless and the prostitutes beside me. Every day someone was dying next to me. I was just a child, but I grew up very fast.

I was ten years old when the Fundación Niños de los Andes took me off the streets and gave me the chance to study and a place to sleep. Now it is six years on. I want to finish my studies, go to university and get money to help my family. I have three small brothers and I don't want them ever to live on the streets. Now that I have a future, I want to work with street childen who don't yet know they have a future."

Alberto Granada, 17, Colombia

The right to education

ARTICLE
26
MADE SIMPLE

Everyone has the right to education, and elementary education shall be free and compulsory for all. Technical and professional education shall be generally available, and higher education available to all on the basis of merit. Parents have the right to choose the education they want for their children, but all education must strengthen respect for human rights and promote the values of peace, tolerance, understanding and friendship between nations.

Even though we don't always enjoy every aspect of school, we all agree it's a good thing! 'Education for all' has only been taken seriously since the 1950s, with the end of colonialism and the advent of independence in the developing world. School enrolment doubled in one generation. Nowadays, most governments world-wide are increasing resources for education. The situation is improving, but exclusion from education by barriers of language, tribe, caste, religion, economic class and geography continues.

Power for girls

Education for girls is vital, but discrimination still goes on. Experts have found that education of women is a vital factor in the elimination of poverty. But among children not attending school, there are twice as many girls as boys, and women make up 60% of all illiterates, or people who can't read or write. As you can see, there is still a long, long way to go.

'Going to school' by Aya Balde, Democratic Republic of the Congo

Illustration by Srijana Shrestha, 15, Nepal

Education in Balochistãn

In Balochistãn, part of Pakistan, there is an acute shortage of female teachers because most adult women in the area have not been eduated properly. Parents, however, only want their daughters to be taught by women, and so they are reluctant to send their daughters to school. This means that girls still don't receive a decent education. The Balochistãn Primary Education Programme was set up to address this problem; it does this by letting the parents choose young women from the village to be trained as teachers. Parents then feel much happier sending their children to school and also show more interest in the benefits of education. In villages where these schools have been set up, 80–100% of the girls now attend school. A way has been found to respect the villagers' right to retain their own culture whilst at the same time giving their young girls the right to education.

Culture and copyright

ARTICLE
27
MADE SIMPLE

Everyone has the right to participate freely in the cultural life of the community, to enjoy the arts, and to share in and benefit from scientific advances. Equally, everyone has the right to protect the copyright of their scientific, literary or artistic work.

What is culture?

Culture is the life-blood of a nation – its music, literature, film, theatre and fashion. There is a danger now that TV and music from the richest countries, with all the marketing and hype they receive, will wipe out smaller national cultures. When a nation loses its life-blood, its heart stops beating, so we have a duty to keep alive the cultures of small nations.

What is copyright?

If you write the world's greatest rock song, you don't want someone else to say that it was their idea and pocket all the proceeds. By owning the copyright, you protect your work; you can copyright anything you write. Similar protection for an object you invent is called a patent. In some countries, these ownership laws are not well respected, as the following story shows.

Ripping off the Rainforest

The tourist in jeans and sunglasses watched as the man in the loincloth heated a sliver of bark over an open fire. He saw him scrape off the bubbles of paste with a dry twig and spread them on the child's wound. Almost at once the bleeding stopped and a film of new skin spread across it.

Later, on the plane, the tourist looked at the sample of paste in front of him and wondered where his friend in the loincloth would sleep tonight? Probably on a bed of leaves. He thought of his own house with the two cars in the garage, the big-screen TV and the warm, comfortable bed, and he wondered, 'Is this fair?'

In the boardroom, the managing director congratulated him on the wonder drug. "This is going to make us millions!" he cried. "I know," said the man, "But can't we give some of it to the forest people who taught us how to make it?"
"What do they need money for? To buy a new loincloth?! Ha! Ha! Ha!" The laughter echoed hollowly in the man's ears as he crept away, feeling like a thief.

A small group of the editors of this book wrote this story together.

Painting by Arshak Sarkissian, 16, Armenia

A free and fair world

ARTICLE

28

MADE SIMPLE

Everyone is entitled to a social and international order in which the rights and freedoms set forth in this Declaration can be fully realized.

If we all wrote down three things that would make a free and fair world, where all rights can be fully realized, everyone's lists would be different. But all of the editors working on this book agree on this point – that every human being has the right to live in peace and security without fear of war or oppression from any other race or nation. At the moment there are around 40 wars taking place, each of which kills more than 1,000 people a year. Most of these victims are not soldiers. War wipes out all human rights – peace is the top priority!

We, children of the tragedy,
We bear inside undressable wounds.
We bear a history of dehumanized humanity
In Algeria or in Bosnia, in Rwanda or Uganda...
How many are we? Tens, thousands...
Lives of whom have been assassinated,
Dreams of whom have been stolen,
Rights of whom have been violated.
We live in a city where there is confusion,
Where the blood flows,
Where horror and terror are sown,
Where arbitrariness is as powerful as the law.

We, children of the tragedy,
We need to be relieved,
To be protected, loved and guided...
We bear inside the fate of Humanity,
Dare to transform our tragedy
Into a symphony of peace and fraternity.
At least respect the declarations you signed,
The Human Rights Declaration is an eternal guide.
Mohammed, 18, Algeria

'I'm too young to die' by Ella Hewitt, 10, UK

Child soldiers

Here is a chilling story we heard from Uganda. The Lord's Resistance Army, an armed opposition group, brainwashes boy soldiers to kill in the name of the Lord. Isaac Odoch is 14 or 15 – he doesn't know. He's now training to be a carpenter at a trauma centre for former child soldiers, but at the age of six, he was snatched from his mother and forced to fight with the rebels.

After military training, Isaac was sent on a mission of brutality and terror. For nine years he was made to roam the land in search of people to murder, kidnap and rape. This horror was all in the name of a holy war to establish a new state based on the values of the Old Testament of the Bible.

ARTICLE
28
MADE SIMPLE

A **free** and **fair** world

In the territory of South Ossetia

The town of Ts'khinvali lies in South Ossetia, between the Black and the Caspian Seas in Asia. War broke out there in January 1992. This is the account of one girl's experiences.

" I was a little girl of about eight when the war began. At first we were not afraid because we couldn't believe that war could really happen. Next morning, the streets of Ts'khinvali were full of policemen and citizens with automatic guns. It was terrible. At night, the houses burned. Nobody could do anything. We were helpless. My mother hid us under the bed. I looked at my parents and saw fear in their faces. I could hear only one word – 'War!'

The town had always been friendly. Many nationalities lived together happily – Russians, Ossetians, Georgians, Armenians and Jewish people. My best friend was called Georgi. We played together and loved each other very much. One day I heard a terrible explosion. I was told that Georgi had been killed at home by his father's grenades. I cried bitterly. We left three days later, with tears in our eyes.

Children don't need grenades, bombs and guns. Children want to be happy with their parents and friends. They need blue sky, sunshine and freedom. I don't want anybody to die. Children must have the right to be free and to study without their schools and homes being bombed. I have no desire to hear bombs and see children dying. Never!! Nowhere!!! "

Anonymous, South Ossetia

Illustration
anonymous, UK

The pit

"*I went to Hagar, near Bihać, to visit a pit called by the local people the 'Abyss', or the 'infinite pit'. During the aggression in my country, the Serbs have thrown around 300 people into the pit. Only half have been identified. I stare at the pit. It is terrible! It is awful! The infinite pit...*"

The infinite pit, the infinite pit,
Feelings are frozen, time has stopped.
Instead of flowers,
Scattered bones on the fields.
You can hear laughter and happiness
Only as inarticulate screams of pain,
Suddenly everything is closed, buried.
Life and time and laughter and
Happiness and tears.
Somewhere inside the people
There is a flame of fear,
Restlessness and darkness.
I am ashamed to be a human being,
That I am born and that I am living.
If we were hyenas
We would have more mercy,
Humanity and sense.
Rights?! Who is talking about rights?!
What are they? Do they exist at all?
I was a child, I was happy.
I was a human being
And I was happy to be alive,
To be able to grow up.
I wanted to leave descendents,
To contribute to the development
Of the human race.
Now I ask myself, does it make sense?
Or did the sense in living disappear
The moment a dozen children,
Men and women were killed,
When people into the infinite...
Into the infinite pit were thrown.
I was a child!
They interrupted my childhood!
I ran after the butterflies,
But I caught up with the killers!

Jasmin Salkic, 17, Bosnia-Herzegovina

Picture by Emma Crake, UK

Our responsibilities

ARTICLE
29
MADE SIMPLE

Everyone has a duty to support and serve his/her community. The law may limit an individual's rights in order to protect the rights and freedoms of others and to ensure the general welfare of democracy. None of these rights may be used in ways that are contrary to the purposes of the United Nations.

We think this Article means that we are all responsible for making sure that each other's rights are protected. These rights weren't written for only important people to worry about. No, it is also up to ME and YOU. It's amazing: if we look back at the end of each day, we realize that every step we take contributes to the future, to better standards of life and to greater freedom. We have an obligation to make choices that do not harm anyone and to respect the universal code of conduct.

'Shopping' by Jantien Roozenburg, 15, The Netherlands

How is a rug made?

Has someone you know bought a rug recently? Does it show the 'Rugmark'? Children in many countries are sold into bonded labour, and made to work for a few pennies a week. Many of them make our carpets and rugs! It matters little to the bosses that the children work 16 hours a day, or that their hands are subject to premature arthritis. The Indian government, in response to public pressure, created a 'Rugmark', awarded only to those carpets and rugs that are made without child labour.

This sounds a great idea but Anti-Slavery International found one problem. There needs to be an independent monitoring system that allows public inspectors to go into any factory at any time to ensure that no children are working there. Otherwise, the Rugmark system is wide open to abuse and corruption.

Next time that you or your family buy a rug or a carpet, look for the mark. Don't take part in this vicious circle of child labour.

Make the right choice

When you go shopping, don't leave your brains behind! It's not just rugs: all sorts of goods – footballs, clothes, shoes, coffee – are produced cheaply through exploitation of workers. Most of us don't know, or even don't care. It's time we realized that you can't rip people off just because they are poor. Everyone, as a consumer, can choose to buy goods that give workers a fair deal. So use your choice.

The vegetables on our plates

Growing exotic foods to sell to wealthy countries often means that the local population is unable to grow the food that they need to live on. Ica, in Peru, is such a place. Most local farmland is used to grow asparagus to sell to the West. In January 1998, Ica's river burst its banks, destroying most of the fields. This meant that there was not enough work for all the people, and the asparagus companies were able to pay them even less than before. The daily wage dropped from 7 soles (a little over US$2) to 5 soles – for a twelve-hour day in the hot sun! Why should these people suffer to provide us with these luxury items? Who's responsible?

Game of football?

66 *Football has always been one of my favourite sports. I love choosing new footballs. One day I was lucky enough to visit the city of Sialkot, in Pakistan. All types of bats, balls and gloves that are used all over the world are produced here. But the most famous product is the football! I visited the leading factory and saw millions of very high-quality footballs; then I came across young children stitching patches of leather. Their hands were filthy and pierced with holes from the needles, and their eyes were red and watering because of the fumes released by the machinery. The whole factory was full of children stitching with all their might. They were aged between 6 and 15.* 99

Zulfiqar Ali Mahar,
14, Pakistan

'Footballer' by Sanid Zuko, 18,
Bosnia-Herzegovina

Don't get me wrong!

ARTICLE
30
MADE SIMPLE

Nothing in this Declaration can be used as an excuse for any person or group to do things that might endanger the rights and freedoms of others.

We all agree that the Declaration is brilliant BUT we noticed that it can seem to contradict itself. Sometimes, you can manipulate Articles to allow you to do exactly the opposite of what another Article intends. For example, you could quote Article 19 as an excuse for making racist remarks. "I'm using my right to free expression!" you claim. But you are also being discriminatory (Article 2) and exercising a right contrary to the spirit of the United Nations (Article 29). If everyone abused Article 22, we would all sit back and rely on others to look after us. And Article 15 would seem to give anyone the right to choose their nationality, requiring the US, for example, to give US citizenship to anyone who wanted it – something they could never do.

So the Universal Declaration must be read with a little common sense. "Do as you would be done by" is at the heart of it, but this is a fragile concept. Many people don't pay any attention to it, but the day that we all do, when we treat people fairly and honestly, and protect them with a good system of policing and law, is the day that we will all live in a peaceful and ordered world.

Do you think the Universal Declaration should be enforced?

Alexander Solzhenitsyn, a Russian writer, spent eight years in a prison camp after he was falsely accused of a political crime.
❝ The best document the UN put out in all its existence was the Universal Declaration of Human Rights, yet it did not even try to make endorsement of it an obligatory condition of membership. Thus it left ordinary people at the mercy of governments often not of their choosing. ❞
Alexander Solzhenitsyn

John le Carré, an English writer famous for his spy stories, believes in the huge potential of the Universal Declaration.
❝ In the future, I imagine the UN being able to interpose itself between belligerents. I believe there should be a clearly defined limit upon the powers of a national government to inflict misery or hardship on their own citizens, whether this means interceding in Iraq on behalf of the Marsh Arabs and the Kurds, or in Russia on behalf of Muslim minorities. ❞
John le Carré

The Universal Declaration is there to protect you – use it, don't abuse it.

Picture by Fabet, Mexico

Opposite: painting by Agne Petiaityte, 12, Lithuania

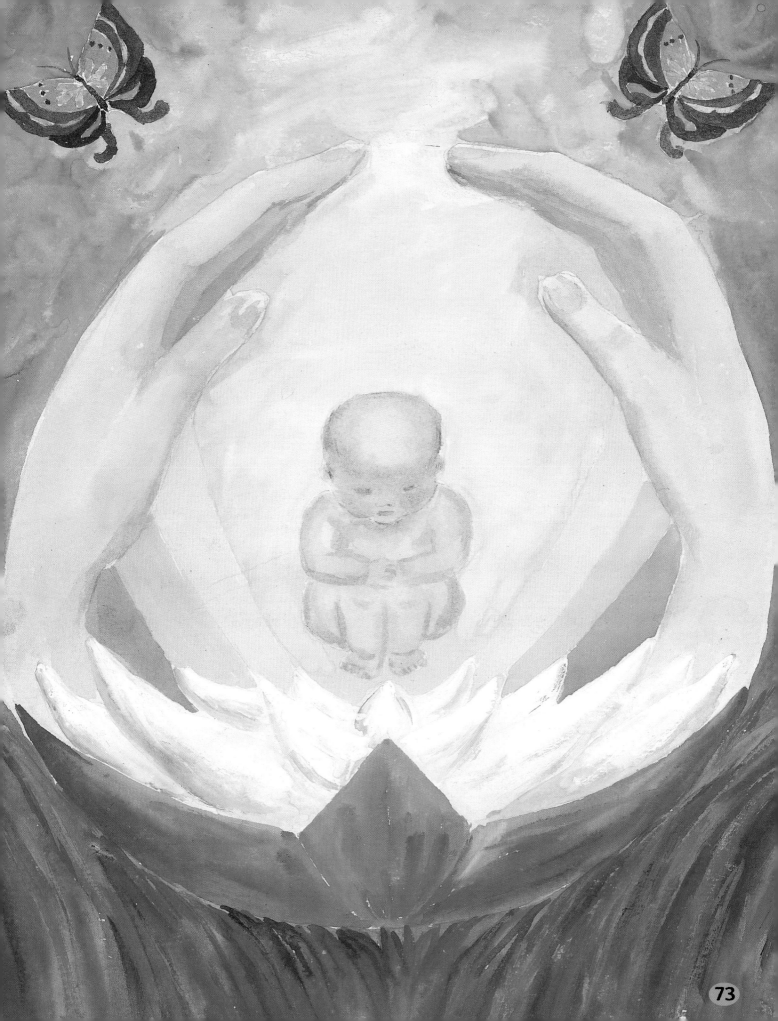

Great Declaration...
...but what are **we** doing about it?

What you can do
Ways the world has devised to protect
our individual rights
– and what you can do to help!

Opposite: painting submitted by the Human Rights
Education Programme, Pakistan

Who can help?

Behind closed doors

Some years ago, it was generally felt that what a husband did to his wife or children in the privacy of his own home was his business. In the same way, governments could do what they wanted to their citizens in their own country, and no international organization could poke their nose in and tell them what to do. That is now changing. Think about it – if you're being beaten up, it doesn't matter much whether the person doing it to you is a relative, a stranger, or a member of your government; you are still getting hurt, and you want someone to stop the beating, right?!

This is why we have the Universal Declaration of Human Rights. Over the last 50 years, several organizations have worked to make these rights real for everyone, chief amongst them the United Nations. Human rights are at the heart of its activities: the UN drafted the Declaration, along with most human-rights laws. Now, in response to pressure, it is urging governments to accept that it carries more influence in the world – to make sure that your government respects your rights. In support of the UN, there are several hands reaching out to help those whose rights are abused.

We found out what the following organizations did.

Commission for Human Rights

This commission, made up of representatives from 43 governments, meets at the UN to consider individual and group complaints about abuses of human rights. It prepares reports and gives instructions for specially appointed people to investigate. As an intergovernmental body, this is the most powerful arm protecting our human rights.

Regional Courts of Human Rights

In Europe, the Americas and Africa, separate declarations of human rights have been prepared to reflect the historic cultures of the regions. Courts of Human Rights have been set up in Europe and the Americas to hear cases of abuse. Governments often find their procedures more acceptable than those of distant international bodies. The European Court in particular has made some very dramatic decisions criticizing the British and other governments.

International Criminal Courts

You may have heard about the prosecution of war criminals by courts set up to deal with the problems in former Yugoslavia and Rwanda. As we finished this book, we heard the great news that a permanent International Criminal Court is to be set up. It will have independent prosecutors who can bring before it any tyrant who is oppressing their people. No longer will the tyrants you have read about go free and unpunished.

Committees looking after Conventions

Various Conventions, including the Convention on the Rights of the Child, each have a special Committee set up to look after them. These Committees require governments who have ratified the Convention to report to them on how well they are complying with the Conventions. If you think your government should be doing more, you can write to the United Nations Commission on Human Rights, Palais des Nations, CH-1211, Geneva, Switzerland, and they will investigate.

UN High Commissioner for Human Rights

The Office of the High Commissioner for Human Rights is the body that works to improve human-rights laws, to encourage more governments to agree to them, and to promote education about them. The current High Commissioner is Mary Robinson.

Illustration anonymous, Pakistan

Time to join in...

...and protect our human rights and the rights of others.

Most people have heard of Amnesty International, but there are lots of other groups out there working away on a daily basis to protect the rights of people who are in no position to do so themselves. Here are just a few of the many groups that we know of. Join one of them or find out which other groups are working in your area!

Article 12

Article 12 of the Convention on the Rights of the Child (CRC) states that all children capable of making up their minds will have the right to express an opinion on matters that concern them. In the UK, Article 12 is an organization run for young people by young people to ensure that whatever their age, they help decide on what happens in their schools, have a say in local community issues, and are allowed to listen in when plans are being made about their future. These are fundamental rights for children. Article 12 protects them!

Contact: 8 Wakley Street, London EC1V 7QE, UK
email: info@article12.uk.com
Website: www.article12.uk.com

Anti-Slavery International (ASI)

Anti-Slavery International was founded in 1839 and is the world's oldest international human-rights organization. ASI campaigns for the freedom of millions of people world-wide who are trapped in situations of slavery or slavery-type practices. It campaigns against: exploitation of child labour; commercial sexual exploitation of children, particularly when connected with tourism; abuse of migrant workers who are trapped and exploited by their employers; bonded labour; early and forced marriage of women and children; trafficking of women for sexual exploitation and all forms of forced prostitution; forced labour; the illegal recruitment of workers by governments, political parties or private individuals, under threat of violence or other penalty; exploitation of indigenous peoples for their labour, land and other resources.

Contact: The Stableyard, Broomgrove Road, London SW9 9TL, UK
email: antislavery@gn.apc.org

AFAPREDESA

Since the Moroccan occupation of Western Sahara in 1976, many Saharawi people have been imprisoned without trial, tortured and kept in horrendous conditions. Lots of organizations exist to support them, particularly in Spain. One, called AFAPREDESA, works collecting and publicizing information about violations of human rights. AFAPREDESA also adopts prisoners or those who have 'disappeared', and asks the Moroccan government officials about their fate and their whereabouts. Its members also participate in an annual student march to Western Sahara to draw attention to the plight of the nation, and to bring hope to its people by showing that others care!

Contact: Oficina de AFAPREDESA España
José Ortega y Gasset, 77-2 Piso A
28006 Madrid, Spain
email: afapredesa@derechos.org
Website: www.derechos.org/afapredesa

If you have any problems contacting the organizations on these pages, please get in touch with Peace Child International (see page 96).

Amnesty International
See pages 80–81.

Defence of Children International (DCI)

DCI is a children's-rights organizations founded exclusively to promote and protect the rights of the child. It has grown to become an international network with members in 60 countries. DCI playeda considerable part in the drafting process of the Convention on the Rights of the Child. Today its International Secretariat works closely with 43 other children's-rights organizations to examine whether the Convention is being followed.

Contact: International Secretariat, 1 rue de Varembe, C.P. 88, CH-1211 Geneva 20, Switzerland
email: dci-hq@pingnet.ch
Website: childhouse.uio.no/childrens_rights/ dci-what.html

Children of the Andes

Children of the Andes is a small British charity dedicated to improving the lives of children at risk in Colombia. It funds projects such as a rehabilitation centre for street children and a 'flying doctor' service for children in remote rainforests. It supports Fundación Niños de los Andes, which provides a home, schooling and a future for youngsters who live on the streets of Bogotá. Children and schools are great fund-raisers for this charity. You can help too!

Contact: 4 Bath Place, Rivington Street, London EC2A 3DR, UK
email: info@children-of-the-andes.org
Website: www.children-of-the-andes.org

Christian Aid

Most aid organizations and religious groups fight for human rights because they know that development and prosperity cannot last where there is no strong culture of human rights. As part of its work, Christian Aid campaigns to change the rules that keep poor people poor: international debt and fair trade are key issues.It was at the forefront of the anti-apartheid movement in the 1980s.

Contact: PO Box 100, London SE1 7RT, UK
email: info@christian-aid.org
Website: www.christian-aid.org.uk

Free Tibet Campaign

Forty-eight years ago, 40,000 Chinese troops marched into Tibet and claimed the country as theirs. The Tibetans were deprived of their nationality and many Buddhist monks and nuns were killed while their temples and treasures were destroyed. Organizations have sprung up around the world to campaign against the action of the Chinese – several of them led by famous film stars such as Richard Gere.

Free Tibet Campaign stands up for the Tibetans' right to decide their own future. It is independent of all governments and is funded by its members and supporters. Its aims are that children may return to Tibet in peace and that the Tibetan people may live as they please and speak their own language. The Tibet House Trust exists to relieve the poverty of Tibetans in exile, to provide educational materials in their language and to support the exiled government of the Dalai Lama.

Contact: 1 Rosoman Place, London EC1R OJY, UK
email: tibetsupport@gn.apc.org
Website: www.freetibet.org

International Save the Children Alliance

The International Save the Children Alliance works in over 100 countries world-wide to promote children's rights. Its founder, Eglantyne Jebb (1876–1928), drafted the first ever statement of the rights of the child. A lot of its work involves raising awareness of children's rights among teachers, social workers, politicians and journalists, as well as among children and young people themselves. Increasingly, the Alliance is helping to make sure that children's voices are heard on all matters that affect them.

Contact: 275–281 King Street, London W6 9LZ, UK
email: info@save-children-alliance.org
Website: www.savechildren.or.jp/alliance

Picture by Damien Boltauzer, 13, Canada

Amnesty International

In 1961, a British lawyer called Peter Benenson wrote a newspaper article urging people everywhere to work peacefully for the release of prisoners of conscience, or people who have been imprisoned for speaking their minds. The reaction was immediate: within a month over 1,000 people from all over the world had responded. From this grew an organization that has over a million members in 160 countries. Amnesty International is now the biggest and most important human-rights group in the world! About 400 people work at its International Headquarters in London.

Its members are concerned with all aspects of human rights and use the 30 Articles you've been reading about as the basis for their campaigns. Amnesty International is very independent and has strict principles about accepting donations. A lot of its work is focused on people who have been unfairly imprisoned and those who are being tortured or generally harshly treated.

Amnesty International tries to raise awareness about abuses of human rights because global attention often forces governments into action. It does this in many ways, which include writing letters to prisoners and governments. In many cases, the people who write these letters don't receive replies and never find out whether they got through or not, but their efforts and attention generally do have a positive effect.

If you're going to get angry with authorities, it is vital that you get your facts straight because otherwise you can look incredibly foolish. Amnesty International spends a lot of time ensuring that information is accurate and up to date. The organization is interested in all aspects of children's rights and many of their volunteers are young people, so get involved! Amnesty International Sections exist in most countries in the world. Many have youth networks. To find out more, contact: Amnesty International, Easton Street, London WC1X 8DG, UK. email: amnestyis@amnesty.org Website: www.amnesty.org

Fulford school, UK, prepares for an exhibition about Amnesty International.

Ten tips for human-rights action from Amnesty International

1 Debates. As you read this book, were there any subjects that you felt particularly strongly about? Think of a motion, organize two teams and get debating.

2 Exhibitions. Make an exhibition about how things are made and where the products come from. Amnesty cannot provide you with research material on this, but some of the organizations listed on pages 78–79 will.

3 A human-rights zone. Declare your school, home or local area a 'human-rights zone'. Make sure that everyone within it respects people's rights and knows what their rights are.

4 Drama. Staging plays is a brilliant way of getting across your message. You could put on plays or sketches about the different articles. But remember to invite important decision-makers so that your ideas will have a positive effect.

5 A human-rights mural. Find out if there is a wall near your home that can be decorated with stories of human rights. You may wish to turn it into a history of human rights in your area, so that everyone knows who their local human-rights heroes are.

6 International Days. Celebrate the special days throughout the year that commemorate important groups or events. Here are a few dates for your diary: 8 March – Women's Day; 1 May – International Labour Day; 5 June – World Environment Day; 11 July – World Population Day; 20 November – International Children's Day; 10 December – Human Rights' Day.

7 Human-rights awards. Find out who has been doing great work promoting human rights in your area and present them with an award. Invite everyone you know to the award ceremony, including the local press so that they can spread the good news.

8 A human-rights fair. Organize speakers to give informative speeches, invite local charities to put up displays, and paint posters that tell people about their rights.

9 Letter writing. Get in touch with your local Amnesty International Section and find out how you can help them with their letter-writing campaigns.

10 Videos. Make a video on a specific issue that you are really concerned about. Make sure that you try to show both sides of the story. Once you have finished, organize a showing for your friends and family, or contact a local TV station and see if they will air your video.

Global action

Human rights are not something out there to be defended by grown-ups at the United Nations or by governments. They are values and principles which every single member of society must believe in and fight for – and that includes YOU!!!

Free the Children

Twelve year-old Craig Kielburger was deeply touched when he heard that Iqbal Masih, a boy his age, had been murdered after speaking out against a lifetime of slavery. (See page 27.) When he discovered that 250 million children between the ages of 8 and 14 work in slave-like conditions, he knew he had to take action. He told his friends and organized an international campaign to 'Free the Children'. In the last two years, he has done more to tackle the issue of child labour than many adults. He has raised money for education centres and to buy cows and sewing machines so that families still have an income once their children have stopped working.

Craig reads up on the subject as seriously as if he were an adult, so that he can never be accused of being naïve. "As young people we have learned that knowledge is power. Child labour is a very complex issue but that is no excuse to ignore the problem. Who better than children to feel and understand the needs of other children?" Free the Children is his mission in this world. Join it! Contact: FTC, 16 Thornbank Road, Thornhill, Ontario L4J 2AZ, Canada email: freechild@clo.com

The Global March

Imagine… former child workers and street children from three continents marching to ask for their right to play, dance and go to school. In January 1998 the dream came true as the Global March began in the Philippines, South Africa and Brazil. After marching through their own continents, the three groups met up in Geneva, Switzerland, in June for a Conference on Child Labour. Sophie Scott-Brown reported from Nepal for the BBC: "For me, a twelve year old called Marnder symbolized the problem. She worked 16 hours a day chipping stones to look after her huge family. She said, 'I'd like to go to school but how can I when I have to work?' That summed it up for me! It was a Global March for education, child rights and equal choices for myself and Marnder."

Picture by Jantien Roozenburg, 15, The Netherlands

"I've joined the march to show my support. Life should be a wonderful experience with children learning in schools and living happily with their parents. But this is not true in much of my country and other places in Africa. Many children have to work very hard because of poverty. This Global March should make things better, but if it doesn't, watch out! I'll be back."

Therese, 19, Senegal

"To be honest, I'm angry. I learned about the Declaration of Human Rights at school and I thought that it was signed by all the countries in the world… so how is it possible that we live in a world where millions and millions of children work in terrible conditions? How has this happened? How can adults be so cruel? I care about this problem and I'm here to shout with the other marchers to tell people that it's time to stop writing beautiful declarations and start really doing something."

Andres, 14, Nicaragua

Success stories

Reading this book, you might be thinking, 'Wow, there are so many terrible things happening around the world, but how can I make a difference?' Well, follow the example of the groups on these pages. We were sent many, many stories of what young people and children have done to fight against the abuse of human rights. Here are just a few of them.

KURM is a Kenyan youth group from Nairobi. It has been campaigning on a range of issues including forced marriage and homelessness. This photo shows KURM putting on a play entitled 'Freedom to choose your wife or husband', which they hope will make the audience aware of their own personal freedoms.

Deep in the Amazon jungle, a youth-run environmental group called Misión Rescate-Perú organized a series of workshops about the Universal Declaration as part of the preparations for this book. The children had the chance to speak their mind about what human rights meant to them. They drew pictures for each of the Articles and put them on display in an exhibition.

In Pristina, groups such as the Kosovo Postpessimists encourage young people to fight for human rights. They focus their activities around the media and journalism to show how human rights are violated in Kosovo. They hope to use their experiences to make other people aware of what their rights are and what they really mean.

Peace Child Algeria has been very active in promoting human rights in its area. Its members have held meetings with young people in Berber and Arabic to discuss equality and violations of human rights in their country. They produced a whole series of poems about the human-rights situation in Algeria.

NATURE is an association in Afghanistan of 2,000 young people involved in different human-rights projects. They have set up a youth forum to work with disabled and orphaned children. NATURE has also created a youth TV programme which highlights the problems facing young people and children in Afghanistan. This photo shows members of NATURE meeting with a UN Special Rapporteur on Human Rights for Afghanistan.

A UNESCO-associated school from Viersen in Germany took part in the Global March against Child Labour in Bonn. They gathered together paintings of feet from 1,500 pupils, along with messages for their political leaders. A group of handicapped children, who couldn't draw their feet, took photos so that they could show their solidarity with the Global March.

Making great strides...

Most of the pupils at the George Mitchell School in East London, England, are from families of Asian, African or Caribbean backgrounds. Some are asylum seekers. In 1995 a twelve year-old Somali refugee, who had been bullied, got into trouble for fighting back in the playground. The school changed what started off as a problem into a positive experience for everyone. His class decided to find out more about refugees and how schools treat them. They met asylum seekers, visited the House of Commons, and made videos. They also wrote a play, which they have performed on various occasions. The project, called 'WHY?', is still going on. The students have gained self-confidence, knowledge about refugees, and the realization that they have a lot to offer. They have done two further projects, one on homelessness and one on bullying. The school is buzzing!

Global Kids Inc. works with young people in New York City, encouraging them to become community leaders and responsible citizens. One of its projects focuses on homelessness both in the city and around the world. The teenagers have just produced the Global Kids Empowerment Book. For a year they developed relationships with legal advisers, policy makers and homeless people. They did research, produced two videos and have given many presentations to help break down stereotypes and make young people more aware of homelessness. So if you are concerned about this issue and want to make a change in your community, this is the book for you!

Picture by Zarin Hasan, Pakistan

... into the future

Well, now that you have read this book, what do you think? Do you feel positive about the future? What will the world be like in 50 years' time? Will everybody know about the Universal Declaration or will it be collecting dust in people's attics? Will our rights be respected? Will torture, slavery and war still exist?

We can all dream and we can all hope, but hoping and dreaming are never as good as doing. As we were writing this book, it became obvious that human rights are not about other people, but about the way we live our lives. And if we use the Universal Declaration as a guide, we're sure that the world will become a better place.

The non-violent activist Gandhi once said, "If ever you have a doubt about which course of action to take, remember the humblest most poor person you have ever seen and ask yourself which course of action would help him the most. The right course of action will immediately become clear to you." We think this is a cool philosophy. When you get out of bed, tomorrow and every day for the rest of your life, think about it...

Illustration by Urjana Shrestha, 18, Nepal

The reference section
Helping you get the information you need

Find your way around the world of human rights

Opposite: illustration by Sarah Wilson, 17, UK

The Universal Declaration

1. All human beings are born free and equal in dignity and rights. They are endowed with reason and conscience and should act towards one another in a spirit of brotherhood.

2. Everyone is entitled to all the rights and freedoms set forth in this Declaration, without distinction of any kind, such as race, colour, sex, language, religion, political or other opinion, national or social origin, property, birth or other status. Furthermore, no distinction shall be made on the basis of the political, jurisdictional or international status of the country or territory to which a person belongs, whether it be independent, trust, non-self-governing or under any other limitation of sovereignty.

3. Everyone has the right to life, liberty and security of person.

4. No one shall be held in slavery or servitude; slavery and the slave trade shall be prohibited in all their forms.

5. No one shall be subjected to torture or to cruel, inhuman or degrading treatment or punishment.

6. Everyone has the right to recognition everywhere as a person before the law.

7. All are equal before the law and are entitled without any discrimination to equal protection of the law. All are entitled to equal protection against any discrimination in violation of this Declaration and against any incitement to such discrimination.

8. Everyone has the right to an effective remedy by the competent national tribunals for acts violating the fundamental rights granted him by the constitution or by law.

9. No one shall be subjected to arbitrary arrest, detention or exile.

10. Everyone is entitled in full equality to a fair and public hearing by an independent and impartial tribunal, in the determination of his rights and obligations and of any criminal charge against him.

11. (1) Everyone charged with a penal offence has the right to be presumed innocent until proved guilty according to law in a public trial at which he has had all the guarantee necessary for his defence. (2) No one shall be held guilty of any penal offence on account of any act or omission which did not constitute a penal offence, under national or international law, at the time when it was committed. Nor shall a heavier penalty be imposed than the one that was applicable at the time the penal offence was committed.

12. No one shall be subjected to arbitrary interference with his privacy, family, home or correspondence, nor to attacks upon his honour and reputation. Everyone has the right to the protection of the law against such interference or attacks.

13. (1) Everyone has the right to freedom of movement and residence within the borders of each state. (2) Everyone has the right to leave any country, including his own, and to return to his country.

14. (1) Everyone has the right to seek and to enjoy in other countries asylum from persecution. (2) This right may not be invoked in the case of prosecutions genuinely arising from non-political crimes or from acts contrary to the purposes and principles of the United Nations.

15. (1) Everyone has the right to a nationality. (2) No one shall be arbitrarily deprived of his nationality nor denied the right to change his nationality.

16. (1) Men and women of full age, without any limitation due to race, nationality or religion, have the right to marry and to found a family. They are entitled to equal rights as to marriage, during marriage and at its dissolution. (2) Marriage shall be entered into only with the free and full consent of the intending spouses. (3) The family is the natural and fundamental group unit of society and is entitled to protection by society and the State.

17. (1) Everyone has the right to own property alone as well as in association with others. (2) No one shall be arbitrarily deprived of his property.

18. Everyone has the right to freedom of thought, conscience and religion; this right includes freedom to change his religion or belief, and freedom, either alone or in community with others and in public or private, to manifest his religion or belief in teaching, practice, worship and observance.

# of Human Rights

19. Everyone has the right to freedom of opinion and expression; this right includes freedom to hold opinions without interference and to seek, receive and impart information and ideas through any media and regardless of frontiers.

20. (1) Everyone has the right to freedom of peaceful assembly and association. (2) No one may be compelled to belong to an association.

21. (1) Everyone has the right to take part in the government of his country, directly or through freely chosen representatives. (2) Everyone has the right of equal access to public service in his country. (3) The will of the people shall be the basis of the authority of government; this will shall be expressed in periodic and genuine elections which shall be by universal and equal suffrage and shall be held by secret vote or by equivalent free voting procedures.

22. Everyone, as a member of a society, has the right to social security and is entitled to realization, through national effort and international co-operation and in accordance with the organization and resources of each State, of the economic, social and cultural rights indispensable for his dignity and the free development of his personality.

23. (1) Everyone has the right to work, to free choice of employment, to just and favourable conditions of work and to protection against unemployment. (2) Everyone, without any discrimination, has the right to equal pay for equal work. (3) Everyone who works has the right to just and favourable remuneration ensuring for himself and his family an existence worthy of human dignity, and supplemented, if necessary, by others means of social protection. (4) Everyone has the right to form and to join trade unions for the protection of his interests.

24. Everyone has the right to rest and leisure, including reasonable limitation of working hours and periodic holidays with pay.

25. (1) Everyone has the right to a standard of living adequate for the health and well-being of himself and of his family, including food, clothing, housing and medical care and necessary social services, and the right to security in the event of unemployment, sickness, disability, widowhood, old age or other lack of livelihood in circumstances beyond his control. (2) Motherhood and childhood are entitled to special care and assistance. All children, whether born in or out of wedlock, shall enjoy the same social protection.

26. (1) Everyone has the right to education. Education shall be free, at least in the elementary and fundamental stages. Elementary education shall be compulsory. Technical and professional education shall be made generally available and higher education shall be equally accessible to all on the basis of merit. (2) Education shall be directed to the full development of the human personality and to the strengthening of respect of human rights and fundamental freedoms. It shall promote understanding, tolerance and friendship among all nations, racial or religious groups, and shall further the activities of the United Nations for the maintenance of peace. (3) Parents have a prior right to choose the kind of education that shall be given to their children.

27. (1) Everyone has the right freely to participate in the cultural life of the community, to enjoy the arts and to share in scientific advancement and its benefits. (2) Everyone has the right to the protection of the moral and material interests resulting from any scientific, literary or artistic production of which he is the author.

28. Everyone is entitled to a social and international order in which the rights and freedoms set forth in this Declaration can be fully realized.

29. (1) Everyone has duties to the community in which alone the free and full development of his personality is possible. (2) In the exercise of his rights and freedoms, everyone shall be subject only to such limitations as are determined by law solely for the purpose of securing due recognition and respect for the rights and freedoms of others and of meeting the just requirements of morality, public order and the general welfare in a democratic society. (3) These rights and freedoms may in no case be exercised contrary to the purposes and principles of the United Nations.

30. Nothing in this Declaration may be interpreted as implying for any State, group or person any right to engage in any activity or to perform any act aimed at the destruction of any of the rights and freedoms set forth herein.

Article 1: The Convention defines a child as a person under 18 unless national law recognizes that the age of majority is reached earlier.

Article 2: All the rights laid down in the Convention are to be enjoyed by children regardless of race, colour, sex, language, religion, political or other opinion, national, ethnic or social origin, property, disability, birth or other status.

Article 3: All sections concerning the child should be in her/his best interests.

Article 4: The State's obligation to translate the rights of the Convention into reality.

Article 5: The State should respect the rights and responsibilities of parents to provide guidance appropriate to the child's capacities.

Every child has:

Article 6: The right to life.

Article 7: The right to a name and a nationality and, as far as possible, the right to know and to be cared for by her/his parents.

Article 8: The right to protection of her/his identity by the State.

Article 9: The right to live with her/his parents unless incompatible with her/his best interests. The right, if desired, to maintain personal relations and direct contact with both parents if separated from one or both.

Article 10: The right to leave and enter her/his own country, and other countries, for purposes of reunion with parents and maintaining the child-parent relationship.

Article 11: The right to protection by the State if unlawfully taken or kept abroad by a parent.

Article 12: The right to freely express an opinion in all matters affecting her/him and to have that opinion taken into account.

Article 13: The right to express views, and obtain and transmit ideas and information regardless of frontiers.

Article 14: The right to freedom of thought, conscience and religion, subject to appropriate parental guidance.

Article 15: The right to meet together with other children and join and form associations.

Article 16: The right to protection from arbitrary and unlawful interference with privacy, family, home and correspondence, and from libel and slander.

Article 17: The right of access to information and materials from a diversity of sources and of protection from harmful materials.

Article 18: The right to benefit from child-rearing assistance and child-care services and facilities provided to parents/guardians by the State.

Article 19: The right to protection from maltreatment by parents or others responsible for her/his care.

Article 20: The right to special protection if s/he is temporarily or permanently deprived of her/his family environment, due regard being paid to her/his cultural background.

Article 21: The right, in countries where adoption is allowed, to have it ensured that an adoption is carried out in her/his best interests.

Article 22: The right, if a refugee, to special protection.

Article 23: The right, if disabled, to special care, education and training to help her/him enjoy a full life in conditions which ensure dignity, promote self-reliance and a full and active life in society.

Article 24: The right to the highest standard of health and medical care attainable.

the Rights of the Child

Article 25: The right, if placed by the State for purposes of care, protection or treatment, to have all aspects of that placement regularly evaluated.

Article 26: The right to benefit from social security.

Article 27: The right to a standard of living adequate for her/his physical, mental, spiritual, moral and social development.

Article 28: The right to education, including free primary education. Discipline to be consistent with a child's human dignity.

Article 29: The right to an education which prepares her/him for an active, responsible life as an adult in a free society which respects others and the environment.

Article 30: The right, if a member of a minority community or indigenous people, to enjoy her/his own culture, to practise her/his own religion and use her/his own language.

Article 31: The right to rest and leisure, to engage in play and to participate in recreational, cultural and artistic activities.

Article 32: The right to protection from economic exploitation and work that is hazardous, interferes with her/his education or harms her/his health or physical, mental, spiritual, moral and social development.

Article 33: The right to protection from narcotic drugs and from being involved in their production or distribution.

Article 34: The right to protection from sexual exploitation and abuse.

Article 35: The right to protection from being abducted, sold or trafficked.

Article 36: The right to protection from all other forms of exploitation.

Article 37: The right not to be subjected to torture or degrading treatment. If detained, not to be kept with adults, sentenced to death nor imprisoned for life without the possibility of release. The right to legal assistance and contact with family.

Article 38: The right, if below 15 years of age, not to be recruited into armed forces nor to engage in direct hostilities.

Article 39: The right, if the victim of armed conflict, torture, neglect, maltreatment or exploitation, to receive appropriate treatment for her/his physical and psychological recovery and reintegration into society.

Article 40: The right, if accused or guilty of committing an offence, to age-appropriate treatment likely to promote her/his sense of dignity and worth and her/his reintegration as a constructive member of society.

Article 42: The right to be informed of these principles and provisions by the state in which s/he lives.

Note: The Convention has 54 Articles in all. Articles 41 to 54 are concerned with its implementation and entry into force.

The Convention on the Rights of the Child was adopted by the United Nations General Assembly 20 November 1989.

Summary by Save the Children Fund/UNICEF

Jargon buster

abolition Getting rid of customs, laws and rules.

aboriginal People who have lived in a place from the earliest known period.

abortion An operation to end a pregnancy.

amnesty A general pardon for people who have been accused of an offence.

Amnesty International An organization that was set up to monitor abuses of human rights.

Anti-Slavery International An organization trying to put an end to slavery.

apartheid The system that the South African government used for keeping apart people of different races.

arbitrary Depending on someone's personal idea or prejudice.

asylum A safe place where people can go.

autonomy The right for a group of people to govern themselves.

Berlin Wall The barrier which used to separate East and West Germany.

bias A prejudice against something.

bonded labour Where a child is 'sold' to an employer in exchange for a loan of money to the family.

boycott Decision by a group of people, government or organization to refuse to deal with a particular person or group.

caste In Hindu society children are born into a certain class or caste.

child labour Where children have to work to earn a living.

citizenship A person's behaviour as a citizen.

civil rights The personal rights of an individual.

civil war War between different groups of people in the same country.

colonialism Where a powerful country takes control of a weaker country or region.

communism A classless society where the State or the community, not individuals, owns property, factories and so on.

conscience A person's sense of what is right and what is wrong.

Convention on the Rights of the Child A UN document setting out the rights that all children should have.

copyright Owning an original work, such as a poem, play or piece of music, and controlling who has the right to use it.

coup Sometimes known as a 'coup d'état', this is where a government is suddenly and often violently taken over by a group of people.

criminal Someone who has broken the law.

crusade Christians in the Middle Ages went on these military expeditions to try to recapture the Holy Land from the Muslims.

culture Beliefs, values and customs passed down through generations.

death penalty Where people are punished by being put to death.

democracy Where a government is made up of representatives who have been voted into power by the people.

developing countries Poorer countries which are trying to build up their industries and the goods they produce.

dictator A ruler who runs a country without allowing any opposition. Whatever he says is law!

disability The loss of some of a person's senses or bodily functions, such as the ability to walk, see or hear.

discrimination Unfair treatment of a person or a certain type of people.

divine right of kings Where a king could do as he pleased without taking notice of anyone else.

dowry The system whereby a girl's family has to give money or property to the bridegroom when she marries.

eco-friendly Something that doesn't harm the environment.

economic Concerning money and finance.

education Schooling.

election Where you vote for somebody to represent you.

empire A whole group of countries and people controlled by one country or ruler.

exile A period of time during which a person is forced to live outside his/her country.

fatwah An order, such as a death sentence, made by an important Islamic leader.

female circumcision The removal of the sensitive part of the female genitals for cultural reasons. This is often carried out by untrained people.

gender Describes whether a person is male or female.

genocide The killing of a whole group or race of people.

government The way in which a country is run.

gypsy A race of people, originally from North West India, who are now found all over the world. They like to travel rather than settle in one place.

illiterate Unable to read or write.

income supplement Additional money provided for an individual or family by the State.

independence Freedom from control. When countries get their independence they are no longer ruled by an outside power.

indigenous The original inhabitants of a region or country.

inquisition An effort by the Catholic Church to seek out and punish people who opposed their teachings. The most famous was the Spanish Inquisition.

Iron Curtain The separation of certain Eastern European countries from the rest of Europe by the Soviet Union. This ended in 1989.

Koran The sacred book of Islam.

law A rule of conduct laid down by a controlling authority.

legal process Enforcing law or having a remedy at law.

liberty Freedom from control or constraint.

Magna Carta A defining law which stated that a king must rule justly when dealing with his subjects.

marriage The legal union of a man and a woman.

massacre Murdering hundreds or even thousands of people at one time.

media A collective term for television, radio, cinema and press.

nation A group of people united by a common language, history or culture.

nationality A person's legal status as a member of a certain country.

persecute To treat someone badly, usually because of their race or religion.

political persecution A person treated badly for holding specific political beliefs.

principle A standard or rule of conduct.

prohibited Stopped from doing something.

prostitution The performance of sexual acts for payment.

Index

race A group of people who are considered to have the same roots.

rapporteur Someone who prepares a report of a meeting for a higher body.

referendum A vote taken by the people on a certain issue.

refugee A person who has been forced to flee his or her country.

religion An organized system of beliefs, ceremonies and worship.

revolution A means of radical change which may or may not be violent.

sati An extinct custom whereby an Indian widow would be burned alive on her husband's funeral pyre.

secular Not concerned with religion.

segregate To separate one group of people from another.

skinhead Youths with shaven heads who are often racist.

social security Financial aid given by the State to reduce poverty.

social services The provision by the State of care for the needy.

society The way in which organized groups of people or animals live together.

Taliban A political and military force which controls most of Afghanistan.

trade union An organization formed to look after the rights of working people.

treaty A formal agreement between two or more governments.

tribe A group of people linked by social or cultural ties.

unemployed Unable to find work.

unemployment benefit Money provided by the State to support those out of work.

United Nations (UN) An organization that tries to achieve world peace and foster international co-operation.

Universal Declaration of Human Rights Refer to pages 8 and 90–91.

values Certain beliefs of what is right and what is wrong.

violation The taking away of a person's rights.

vote A means by which to indicate a choice.

World Health Organization (WHO) A United Nations organization to improve health.

Peace Child International

In Papua New Guinea when warring tribes of head-hunters made peace, they gave each other a baby. The children grew up with their new tribes and if, in the future, conflict threatened, the tribes would send these children to resolve it. Such a child was called a 'Peace Child'.

Peace Child International was founded in 1981 to give young people the chance to speak out on issues that are important to them. For the first eight years, the main focus was a musical called 'Peace Child'. It told how young people of warring nations worked together to build peace between their countries through pioneering youth exchanges.

Since 1981 there have been over 5,000 performances of 'Peace Child' in 31 countries, each one unique and each reflecting different youth concerns on global issues. One of the chief concerns has been about environmental issues, and Peace Child International moved into publishing to allow young people to express their concerns on paper. Since 1992, three different environmental publications have been written, illustrated, designed and edited by young people. The most successful is 'Rescue Mission Planet Earth' – a young people's edition of Agenda 21, the plan for the future agreed upon at the Earth Summit in Rio de Janeiro. It was created in the same way as this book and has sold hundreds of thousands of copies in 18 different languages.

Peace Child has close links with the United Nations and works with 500 groups around the world. But what makes it a really unique organization is that young people have a huge role in running it and making decisions about its strategies and projects. The headquarters are in England, where young people from all over the world come and manage projects. And they all live in a hostel designed and built by a 19 year-old Czech student. At Peace Child, we are always open to new ideas and searching for new contacts. We have a quarterly newsletter, written by young people, that is distributed world-wide. So if you have enjoyed this book and would like to be involved, get in touch. Here are the details – now it's up to you.

Peace Child International
The White House, Buntingford,
Herts SG9 9AH, UK
Tel: 44 (0) 1763 274459
Fax: 44 (0) 1763 274460
email: 100640.3351@compuserve.com
Website: www.oneworld.org/peacechild

Peace Child International is a British Registered Charity – No. 284731